RACISM
A DISEASE
OF THE MIND

ADELEKE ADEFIOYE

Racism: A Disease of the Mind

©2020 Adeleke Adefioye

print ISBN: 978-1-09833-668-4

ebook ISBN: 978-1-09833-669-1

CONTENTS

ACKNOWLEDGEMENT

First and foremost, I always like to return all the glory to Almighty God, in whom and through whom we live. Warmest appreciation to my amazing parents, Prince and Mrs. Alfred Adewusi Adefioye, for their daily fervent prayers and to all my siblings–Funke, Yinka, Toyin, and Bukky, my ever sweet baby. Thanks for all of your support individually and collectively. To my adorable niece–Tamilore Omole, a great book lover. Thanks for being uncle's greatest cheerleader.

I'm eternally grateful to Les Lambus for all the inspiration and contribution. Les was not only passionate about the success of this book, he motivated me, supplied materials and showed interest at every stage from concept to production. He cheered this initiative to the finish line. Les—I appreciate you. You are one in a million. Literally.

I specially applaud Jane Elliot, the renowned anti-racism activist and educator, for her consistent fierce fight for racial justice and decades of erudite discussion on race and racism. Your laudable contribution to global peace through anti-racism education has not gone unnoticed. You are an icon and a hero. The entire world appreciates you.

Special thanks to the leadership team and members of Victory Church of O'Fallon, Illinois, for their love and friendship when I was a Lone Ranger. Thank you Victory for being a congregation of love and care. Jon and Debbie Cannon–Thanks for all the ever dependable spiritual leadership and effective Godly guidance. It feels great to be under the tutelage of a leader who leads and listens. I also appreciate Pastor Sandy Adams of Calvary Chapel of Stone Mountain in Atlanta, Georgia. Thanks for feeding me spiritually.

I'm grateful to the management and staff of Stifel Financial Corporation, an incredible firm reputed for excellence and integrity, for all the valuable opportunities. I also appreciate the Book Baby Team for your poised and distinct professionalism.

I say a big thank you to my uncle–Godwin Gbadebo Adefioye. Your selflessness, integrity and impeccable character are exemplary. You are the world's best uncle. I'm indebted to a true friend who I refer to as *sweet sister*—Henrietta Otsu. I appreciate your friendship and time invested in all of the daytime and late night calls. Your contributions during all the virtual strategy sessions are appreciated. Your genuine concern didn't go unnoticed. To my gifted friend—Josephine Osakwe, you are a friend like no other. Thanks for all of those valuable pieces of advice and timely intercessions.

To a jolly good fellow that I nicknamed 'Big Boss' Clay Lumsden–Your selflessness is immeasurable. You're such a great power house with a solid foundation and abundant grace of God. I also appreciate Jim Metzenthin, a rare kind-hearted man and a resourceful professional with an uncommon humility. To all of my professional team members: Chip Steitz, Awais Irfan, Adam Leiweke, Steve Slechta, Dalton Burton, Joseph Padiyara and Adrian Wright. You guys are more than wonderful.

A special appreciation to Dr. Sara Schecter for granting me an interview while working on this book. Your rare kindness is well appreciated. I declare an admiration for a couple that I have so much respect for—Eldon and Barbara Schmidt, I admire your leadership skills.

I would like to express a sincere appreciation to great people whose words of encouragement gave me strength: Tom and Sharon Seibert, your kindness always beats my imagination. Mark and Cherie Ellis, words are not enough to express my appreciation for trusting me even when I was relatively a total stranger. Trinisha Smith, a very selfless friend who admires and celebrates success. I value your gift of friendship more than you could ever imagine. Chief Awosina, a man with an incredible network of influential folks. Sir, I appreciate all of your help placing me in front of the right people at the right time. Godspower Eseh, a man with a big vision. Mykel Board, a man with an indisputable good heart. Mr. Gbadegesin Tony Bamidele, a man with a great wisdom. Mr. Charles Orbih, a man with a great gift of coordination and wise counsel. Ohiole and Emilia Aghomo, a reliable and supportive team (couple-team as I love to refer to them). Dr. Presly Obukoadata, a very good friend who sees the big picture in every concept. Bobbie Clark-Alexander, the strongest independent woman alive. Your resilience always motivates me to do more. Marcia Meadows, a resourceful and kindest manager ever. Jamie Fritz, a gifted and most selfless manager ever. Attorney Steve Ikezahu, my most dependable ally. Reid Ingle, thanks for being there. Celebrating Thanksgiving at your in-laws' still remains indelible in my memory. With a broad smile, I give a wink to Femi Omole, a brother from another mother.

I also appreciate friends who encouraged me at some point: Jose Malave, the great professor. Leslie Ward, Chika Salome Osunkwo, Mary Nwaeke, Bridget Okhiria, Dustin and Talia Sega, Brad and Teri Range, Adam and Tania Evans. (Dustin, Brad and Adam, I specifically appreciate and admire what you guys do in God's vineyard). Eyitayo

Arikenbi, Damaris Montgomery, Chris and Ciara McMillan, Filip and Tiffany Pantovich, Josh and Kerri Riley, Phil and Patty Mullins, Dana Heyde and Ronald Chatelain. I respect and admire you guys.

To all the nice folks whose paths have crossed mine–Steve and Jacquie Junker, Tunji Saliu–ora awe, Harold and Jami Woods, Byron and Kyong Jimerson, Dave and Dawnetta Hornyak, Jodi Templeton, Dan and Kathy Woloszynek Sr., Biodun Fadare, Pat and Linda Albers, Becky Kappert, Dayo Sokan, Bright Olatunji, Sina Agunbiade, Sunny Orbih, Ryan and Connie Denny, Dianne Griffin, Nancy Barnett, Myrna Faye Voellinger, Mercy Omenka, Opeyemi Eluwole, the Albright family—Reynold, Donna, Brandy, Blake and Bailey, management and staff of Daryl L. Kidd, P.C. Family Law Group, Marietta, in Atlanta, Georgia and others too numerous to mention. Thank you all. I'm indebted to you guys for all of your support.

To Simisola and the boys–Dotun, Doyin and Dola.

I love you more than words could ever express.

FOREWORD

Racism: A Disease of the Mind is a moving book that conveys a message of unity, that we are all one. It is a plea against racism and tribalism. It is an advocate for letting love make the world go round rather than allowing hatred and bigotry to essentially destroy the world.

The book contains an analysis of racism and tribalism more thorough and better researched than any I have ever read. The author makes it clear that racism and tribalism exist everywhere. There is racism in the United States, a country of multiple races. In a country of one race, such as Nigeria, the same negative effects are created by tribalism. The two are equivalent. The author studies the concepts philosophically and proves that racism and tribalism make not even a tiny bit of sense.

The book contains some wonderfully lyrical writing. The quotations the author has chosen to start each chapter are apt and inspiring. I wrote several down to keep.

The author has taken on an important, difficult, and complex topic with passion, scholarship, and clarity, and in so doing has produced a wonderful book. I wish the author the best of luck with it.

BookBaby Publishing Team.

PREFACE

Racism is, no doubt, the bane of our existence as humans. God created race, but humans, out of hate, selfishness, and unhealthy rivalry, created racism. Evidently, racism has torn the human race apart. Regrettably, it has also led to brutality, hate, animosity and the incessant civil unrest that we have all witnessed. The primary aim of this book is to promote love, eradicate racial line, ensure a harmonious relationship between the police and the citizens, restore global peace and unite humans.

Adeleke Adefioye.

CHAPTER 1:

I CAN'T BREATHE

It is not our differences that divide us. It is our inability to recognize, accept and celebrate those differences.

– Audre Lorde

All of a sudden, I began to experience an unusual perspiration. A perspiration that altered the rhythm of my heartbeat. The more the rhythm was thrown off, the more rapid my heartbeat pounded. I listened with displeasure as my heartbeat produced discordant tunes. The tunes were unpleasant to the ears.

I held my breath to slow down the pounding rate of my heartbeats. I rearranged the beats in a desperate attempt to make them fall back into a normal sequence. I mentally struck the cords of my heartbeats to force a change. I looked beyond a glaring disruption of my internal body anatomy. I tried to be a man. A man who would not let out an emotion that will make him feel less of a man.

I thought I had seen it all. There's absolutely nothing that'll make me feel less of a man—so I assumed. Unfortunately, my confidence failed me, as did my assumption. My ability failed me, as did my prowess. My strategy failed me, as did my confidence and strength.

Then, my manliness gave way as my eyes responded to involuntary blinks. As my eyes blinked, the tears rolled down my cheeks. I felt the temperature of the tears as they rolled down. They were above warm—close to boiling. The lacrimal glands may have boiled them up as they flowed to the tear ducts. They hurt as they journeyed down my cheeks and dropped on my chest.

Then, all of a sudden, there was a strange feeling. A strange feeling of restoration that reset my heartbeat. A clog in the wheel of my heartbeats slowed the rapid rate. Then, it fell back into a normal sequence. Then, a restoration of rhythm. Then, a normal heartbeat.

I sat and wondered what the emotional roller-coaster was all about. When did I stop being a man? How did I get so tortured over a movie? How could a movie disrupt my internal body anatomy? How could a movie move me so terribly? Funny enough, the movie is very familiar. I'd seen it before now. I paused for a moment as I searched through my mind again. The search confirmed my assertion. The movie is very familiar; so is the title. I know what the title is. I know exactly what the title connotes. The movie is titled *I Can't Breathe.*

Written by Eric Garner and directed by Ahmaud Arbery. Breonna Taylor, Trayvon Martin, Jamar Clark, Philando Castile, Botham Jean, Michael Brown Jr., Ezell Ford, Michelle Shirley, Stephon Clark, Tamir Rice and other talents are cast members. The movie was produced by George Floyd.

I Can't Breathe is adrenaline pumping with no suspense. With smooth transitions between scenes and a predictable end, *I Can't Breathe* is a high-budget movie that happens to be a sequel to itself. All components of the movie are super weird. From effects to visuals. From structure to scenes, and from cinematography to dialogue. They all reflect turpitude and a flagrant disrespect for human dignity on one side, and a shameful brutality that was glaringly excessive on the other. The movie was shot in Minneapolis. Despite being a high-budget movie, it has absolutely no entertainment value. The movie is indeed very familiar; so is the spooky title.

I Can't Breathe interrupted a reality show christened *Covid-19*. The movie flourished in fame like the *Covid-19* show it halted. It began like an interlude with familiar scenes. The first scene lasted for eight minutes, forty-six seconds. A gruesome knee-over-neck scene. The producer shuttled between crew and cast. He was a crew member and also a part of the cast team.

The producer begged to stay alive. The producer struggled to stay alive. The producer clamored for air. The producer hoped for a savior. He yearned for breath—a free gift from his creator.

The knee on his neck never budged. The knee on his neck intensified its grip. The knee had a face of anger and hate. The knee was a designated messenger of death. The knee on his neck…that knee on his neck was on a heinous mission.

The knee had a well-defined job description. The knee went over, above, and beyond to complete its assigned task. Yes, the knee did its job perfectly. It was a cardiopulmonary arrest mission—a brutal assignment carried out in the most devilish style.

In a millisecond, the knee successfully completed a quick troubleshoot that instantaneously identified the producer's neck as the most vulnerable organ. The knee promptly went for it. It blocked the producer's neck and prevented blood flow to his brain. It blocked the producer's neck and prevented airflow to his lungs. And when eight minutes, forty-six seconds were over, so was the producer's life.

As I wiped off the profuse tears and imagined how excruciatingly painful the producer's last minutes of life must have been, I sobbed and hoped I wouldn't get to watch this movie again. *I Can't Breathe* is one tragic movie too many. George Floyd, the producer, and the entire crew as well as the cast all committed a crime and were found guilty of a one-count charge of skin color—a criminal offence punishable by death.

Then, they paid the ultimate price—their lives. Wait a minute! Is it too late to appeal? I thought there was no right that was right enough to take a man's life. I thought there was no wrong that was wrong enough to justify that heinous act. I thought there was only one race—the human race.

CHAPTER 2:

WHAT IS RACISM ABOUT?

Change will not come if we wait for some other person or some other time. We are the ones we've been waiting for. We are the change that we seek.

– Barack Obama

Expectedly, racism is a little hard to define. It is broad. So very broad. The deeper you attempt to go, in an attempt to unfold its meaning, the more confused you become. Past attempts have either ended up as a scratch on the surface or a definite approach from a specific angle. Perhaps it is one of those subjects that fits perfectly into "the more you look, the less you see" cliché.

For instance, in the United States of America, some people tend to draw a line between racism and slavery, while some don't see why either of them should be viewed distinctly. Those who are of the opinion that racism and slavery can't be dissociated from each other have simply argued that while racism is a form of discrimination against people based on race, slavery, in itself, is a form of hostility toward a specific race.

A considerable number of folks whose actions give them away as racists wouldn't want to be seen, identified, addressed or branded as racists for the most part. People in this category tend to define racism in a way that points an accusing finger away from them.

Evidently, slavery played a major role in the events that culminated in secession of the South from the Union, which eventually led to Civil War in the United States, although the South chronicled reasons for secession from states' rights to high tariffs and taxes.

However, a cross-section of scholars and historians have christened these reasons as myths. They argued that the main reason was connected to the fact that the South was at loggerheads with the North. It may be recalled that the North was in favor of the abolishment of slavery.

To some extent, it may be justifiable to treat slavery as racism if the historical antecedent of slavery is anything to go by. However, it is also fair to reason with those who feel slavery and racism are two different social issues that need to be distinctly addressed apart from each other.

This book focuses primarily on racism. For the purpose of a clear focus and consistency, the definition of racism will be evaluated vis-à-vis slavery.

The definition of racism is all over the place. From Merriam-Webster to civil rights activists. From institutional to legal definitions. Some have the notion that racism simply encompasses a belief (heinous or otherwise) that race is solely the major determinant of human abilities, capacities, capabilities and traits. Others believe that racism is when an individual or a group of individuals holds an opinion of human inequality or propagates an ideology of human supremacy based on race. In whole, this is connected to Adolf Hitler's belief of a master race. His infamous declaration of this heinous belief forms the pivot on which the Nazi movement swings.

What, then, is racism? In more plain terms, since this book intends to lay emphasis on the human angle of the subject, racism is prejudice meted out to people based on their race. In line with this definition, discrimination triggered by race automatically qualifies to be labeled as racism.

Over the decades, there have been different ideologies with an undertone of racism. These ideologies range from a determined attempt to divide the human race along the line of race to setting up categories in which human beings are placed based on their race. Simply view racism as the hatred of a certain race by people of another race.

Slavery, on the other hand, if it has to be dissociated from racism, portrays a heinous form of subjugation. It refers to a situation where some portions of property law are applied to people, thereby empowering some individuals either statutorily or by way of privilege due to economic or political power, to purchase other individuals for specific purposes or sell these same individuals for profit.

If I'm saddled with the task of designing a family tree of Mr. Racism, I will make a concerted effort to graphically illustrate that Mr. Stereotype and Mr. Wrong Accusation are his siblings, while Mr. Hate and Mr. Animosity will be depicted as their first cousins. In the same vein, Mr. Slavery's siblings are Mr. Servitude and Mr. Bondage, while Mr. Domination and Mr. Subjection take the place of first cousins.

Come to think of it, just like a journey of a thousand miles begins with a single step, the journey of racism begins with a mental state—a mental state that not only assumes but substitutes hypothesis for proven facts. Being stereotypical is disgusting. It is one of the unfortunate results of the inability to mentally engage oneself in logical reasoning.

Personally, that's what I refer to as mental indolence: solely acting based on impulse triggered by misguided and subjective stimuli. Evidently, logical reasoning and mental indolence play out differently.

CHAPTER 3:

GETTING IT RIGHT

The only way out of the labyrinth of suffering is to forgive.

– John Green

Logical Reasoning Scenario

Dalton is a young man who grew up in a middle-class family. He is unassuming, hardworking and an ardent lover of the system of justice. However, he has a mind of his own. His soft spot for justice eventually influenced his career choice, as he becomes a police officer.

On the other side of town lives another young man. His name is Jamal. He's also from a middle-class family. He's a gentleman with good manners. Like Dalton, Jamal is also very hardworking, with great family values. He also has a mind of his own. His love for technology influenced his career choice as he ends up as a software developer for an investment firm.

One Monday morning, Jamal woke up a little late. For some reason, he didn't hear his alarm go off that fateful morning. He had missed his regular bedtime the previous night as he came back home late from a family event. He knew he had to hurry up, otherwise he would miss his scheduled eight a.m. meeting at the office. It was an important meeting, which had modalities of the final test plan of his team's newly developed software as the main item on the agenda.

His driving was a little off and awkward that morning as he swerved in between lanes in an attempt to beat time. The awkward driving was noticed by Dalton, who was on a routine patrol. He swung into action by following Jamal's car. After cautious and clever maneuvers, Dalton caught up with Jamal and pulled him over.

As Dalton got out of his patrol car, Jamal slightly adjusted the hinged flap of the visor, tilted the mirror a little bit and watched the young officer walk briskly towards him. To him, as briskly as the officer walked, it still appeared to be the longest short distance walk he had ever seen. As he waited almost motionless behind the wheel, his imagination went wild as he began to mentally build a premonition of what the encounter with the officer would be like.

Unfortunately, Jamal didn't have the luxury of time to complete the self-imposed mental process, as a mild tap from Dalton's index finger on the driver's-side window brought his mental process to a halt. As he looked sideways towards the direction where the sound from the tap came from, their eyes met and Dalton, through gesticulation, instructed Jamal to roll down the driver's-side window.

Good morning officer, Jamal greeted politely as he pressed the power window knob. The window rolled all the way, revealing Jamal's full face and his upper body. Dalton, at this time, realized Jamal and himself obviously had different race identities. Jamal had realized that from an earlier gaze at the mirror on the visor.

Good morning sir, Dalton responded. *Do you realize you've been speeding way over the legal speed limit for this area? Are you also aware you've been involved in an indiscriminate change of lanes with little or no regards to your safety and the safety of other drivers and road users?* Dalton queried.

I apologize, officer. I honestly didn't realize that. I'm super late for work and I have an eight a.m. meeting to catch up with, Jamal explained.

I guess that meeting is more important than your life as well as the lives of other road users, Dalton posited sarcastically.

Nope, the meeting is not worth anyone's life. I know you're being sarcastic and I totally agree with you, Jamal responded, lending credence to Dalton's statement.

You literally swerved indiscriminately between lanes in a serpentine form over and over again, Dalton reminded Jamal. *So, how much have you had to drink?* The unassuming officer eventually asked. As a matter of fact, Dalton had been doing this for some time now. He has heard pulled-over drivers give divergent reasons for speeding. From incredible to dumb. From flimsy to mundane and from ridiculous to weird.

Having listened to Jamal's reason, he was a little convinced but still wanted to be sure the weird driving was not as a result of being under some kind of influence. Dalton just didn't want to swallow Jamal's pill hook, line and sinker. It would be devastating to let a drunk driver off the hook, thereby endangering lives—the same lives he had sworn to protect.

Zero. Not even a sip, Jamal simply responded in an attempt to satisfy Dalton's inquisitiveness. *It is too early to drink and besides, I don't even drink at all,* Jamal added, attempting to convince the officer some more that he was definitely not driving under the influence of alcohol.

Could you please step out of the car for me? Dalton ordered politely. He was determined to clear the air himself with some facts.

Jamal complied respectfully. Dalton conducted some sobriety tests, which included breathalyzer, straight-line walk, alphabet recitation and eye-balling a moving object. Jamal passed all the tests.

Lastly and expectedly, Dalton went back to his patrol vehicle to run Jamal's driver's license, which he had earlier collected from him at the time he stepped out of the car. I'm assuming this is part of the training for the officers. They always request your driver's license even if you're pulled over for the most trivial traffic violation that may eventually earn you a mere warning or an outright pardon. So Jamal didn't see any big deal as he handed Dalton his driver's license. Everything came back okay with a clean driving history afterwards.

Satisfied, Dalton walked back to Jamal and handed him his driver's license with no tickets. *Drive safely and be very careful. Please remember there is no meeting that is worth your life or anyone's,* Dalton advised.

I sure will, officer. Thanks," Jamal enthused as he reached for his wallet to return his driver's license.

Afterwards, he inserted the wallet into the right side pocket of the pant he had on, cleared his throat and cranked the engine. As he tried maneuvering his way back on the road, he took a look at his watch to check what the time was. He then realized how super late he was, but was extremely thankful that the officer had either saved him from wrecking his car or causing a major auto accident.

Notes from Logical Reasoning Scenario

For Both Dalton and Jamal

- Dalton and Jamal have different race identities.
- They both have mutual respect for each other.
- They are both not stereotypical.

For Dalton

- An excellent display of professionalism.
- He never, in his mind, prejudged Jamal based on his race.
- His actions throughout the encounter depicts that he treats people as individuals and not according to their race.

For Jamal

- He never assumed he was pulled over based on his race.
- He did not view Dalton as an individual of a certain race but as a law enforcement agent.
- He respectfully followed Dalton's orders.

The Outcome

- There was no altercation.
- There was no ego or bruised ego.
- The encounter ended up being a win-win situation.
- A possible loss of life was prevented.
- A possible auto accident was prevented.
- A peaceful coexistence was enhanced.

CHAPTER 4:

GETTING IT WRONG

Be kind, for everyone you meet is fighting a hard battle.

– Plato

Illogical Reasoning: Mental Indolence Scenario

Brett is a thirty-year-old man. He is the first child of his parents. He grew up on the North Side of town with his two other siblings. Their dad is a practicing Christian. He did a good job instilling Christian values in their minds. Unfortunately, he left out one of the most important Christian values: love.

In addition to the Christian values, Brett's dad also gave his kids a series of life lessons as they grew up. Social interaction was one of the series. Every now and then, he told them about people of a specific race to be avoided. According to him, people of the race in question were a societal menace whose favorite pastime is fomenting trouble and committing crime.

Expectedly, Brett and his siblings grew up with a fully developed mental image—a very subjective mental image—of a race maliciously presented to them by their dad. Every one of them had an individually pre-established specific behavioral pattern for people of this race. They eventually attributed this stereotype to everyone across the board as long as they were people of the race in question.

Long after leaving their parents' home, Brett and his siblings still had special places in their hearts where this stereotype was safely preserved and continually nurtured. Brett eventually became a police officer. From a very tender age, he had always wanted to be a law enforcement agent.

While in high school, he would go to the police department to pick up the latest edition of the department's monthly journal. He never missed any. It was one of the ways he kept himself abreast of all the activities of the local police officers. He read about new tactics in combating crime, crime watch, crime detection and periodic drills for officers. He paid rapt attention in the most focused manner to appointments, promotions, hierarchy, recruitments and administration columns of the journal. He read everything about the police department.

Whenever they had dinner on the family dinner table or out in their favorite restaurants, Brett hardly talked about any topic aside from law enforcement. His parents were always astonished by how much their "little boy" knew about the police department.

He liked the uniform, the branded patrol vehicles, their dispute resolution prowess, the respect they command in the community and the selfless service they offer. As a matter of fact, he liked everything about the police. So Brett's parents and siblings were not, in any way, surprised that he ended up being a police officer. In fact, they would have been very surprised if he had chosen a different career.

Like Brett's family, there is this other family on the other side of town who are people of the race stereotyped by Brett's dad. The name of the first child of the family is Marvin.

Marvin is a 27-year-old man. He is the first child of a family of four. His dad, a retail worker, loves and provides for his family. He was always available while they were growing up. From baseball to basketball practice, from family outdoor events to indoor games, Marvin's dad was always available. He taught all his kids their first lessons about life. One of those life lessons had to do with social interaction outside of the home.

He prepared Marvin's mind as well as the minds of his other siblings for an inevitable reality. He didn't mince words telling them how best to view certain people of a specific race as foes and adversaries. To Marvin and his siblings, dad was a symbol of authority. They believed him and began to see people of the race stereotyped by their dad as enemies. To them, people of this specific race were devilish and satanic, and as a result of this misguided perception, Marvin and his siblings always felt there were scores to settle with these "devilish and satanic" people.

From an adolescent age, Marvin always displayed a unique musical talent. He was everything his dad wasn't in terms of attention to details, music collection and love for rhythm as well as a good ear for beats. At age fifteen, Marvin was already a multi-instrumentalist. He plays the guitar, flute, drums and piano. Amazingly, he thought himself how to play these musical instruments.

For hours, he would lock himself up in his room. By the time he unlocked the door, he would emerge with a pile of sheets of 8½ by 11 paper in his hand. Believe it or not, those pieces of paper would have on them well-arranged lyrics that had the potential of being in the top twenty albums on the billboard chart ranks. For real, Marvin was that good. His parents had noticed the potential in him and did the best they could to help preserve all his original works from when he was a child.

As days rolled into months and months into years, Marvin's talent grew and matured. It was an amazing no-holds-barred kind of talent. In junior and senior high schools, Marvin scooped up various awards as he won all the organized talent shows in and outside of school. Before he finished high school, he had become a local champion and a celebrity of a sort with a long string of awards and accolades.

Shortly after school, Marvin left home in a determined bid to actualize his age-long ambition of becoming a successful recording artist. He moved to a city considered the nerve center of entertainment in every sense of the word. Armed with his demo tapes, he approached a couple of recording companies. He had prepared a list of his dream recording firms long before he left his hometown.

He had not gotten midway into his prepared list when he began to receive invitations for auditions. His first audition was an eye-opener to certain things that he never knew existed in the music industry. Marvin was specifically dazzled at the state-of-the-art equipment inside the studios. It wasn't anything like the mini-studio exclusively set up for him in his parent's basement, nor was it anything like the best studios he had visited within a 100-mile radius of the city he grew up in.

After the first bouts of auditions, Marvin got a great offer for an unbelievable record deal. He didn't have to consult anyone to make a decision about the offer. It was an opportunity-of-a-lifetime kind of offer.

As soon as he signed on the dotted line, the first call he made was to his parents. With a modest pride, he told them about his achievements and how life-changing the deal he got would be. His parents had never been more proud of him. They literally hopped for excitement and congratulated him endlessly with a thunderous ovation. His mom in particular. She danced, danced and then danced until her husband requested to know what music she was dancing to. Apparently, there was no music playing anywhere in the house. It was a dance of joy and excitement, and doesn't require any music for the most part.

This didn't come as a surprise when he called to inform his parents. They'd always known that Marvin would be a huge success someday. They had no idea when it would happen, but they just knew it would happen someday and somehow.

In an attempt to celebrate the deal and obtain his parents' blessings for the kick-off of his musical career, Marvin informed them of his plans to drive home the next day. Again, mom was the first to let Marvin know his plans to come for career kick-off blessings was a great idea. She didn't hang up until she announced to her dear son that she would prepare him his favorite home-cooked meal.

For Marvin and his parents, that night was the longest night ever. Marvin stayed awake for the most part of the night, as he couldn't wait to hug his parents and listen to them tell him how proud they were of him. In the same vein, the parents couldn't wait to have him back home and look straight into the eyes of their once-little boy as his life was about to change.

Since Marvin's parents couldn't fall asleep out of excitement, they decided to use the opportunity for something else. They went straight to what used to be Marvin's room. It was a makeshift room in the basement next to the home studio they had set up for him at the time he completed his elementary school education. They scrubbed, cleaned, dusted and made it habitable again. They replaced the sheets on the bed. They didn't stop at Marvin's old room; they also cleaned other parts of the house in readiness to host their soon-to-be-a-celebrity son.

Marvin hit the road soon after he woke up. Obviously, he'd had a long night and also had to contend with an almost-all-day drive. The excitement of about-to-change life was enough of an antidote to the stress that came with the trip. He made intermittent stops for gas and snacks—one of the habits he picked up from his dad.

Marvin's dad would snack in between everything all day. He kept repositories of snacks everywhere. At home, at work, in the car. Everywhere. He would snack in between meals, tasks, phone calls—literally in between everything. Weird enough, every time he woke up to use the bathroom in the middle of the night, he would snack on either nuts or cookies before going back to bed.

Like his dad, Marvin was also huge on snacks. Not as addicted as his dad, though. As he drove home, Marvin couldn't get his mind off the fact that his life was about to change. For years, he had fantasized about the opportunity he just had. He was confident that his first album would no doubt be a huge commercial success. He began to mentally draw up a list of the things he would do for his parents. By the time he was done, buying a house for his parents in one of the choice areas of town was topmost on the list.

They deserve it, he reasoned, justifying his action. That was exactly true, though. As a family, they'd gone through several bouts of hard times. They had pulled through a total of three evictions in the past. For several nights, they went to bed hungry, with no assurance of the next day's meal. His dad's meagre income working at a small retail store was never enough to sustain them.

Marvin remembered how he would either show up late to baseball practice or show up two hours before schedule because they always had to take the bus to get around. He also remembered all the sacrifices his parents made for him and his other siblings—especially how his dad took a loan to set up the home studio for him. *He must have believed so much in me.*

Finally, Marvin drove into town. His phone rang just at about the time he brought it out to call his parents. It was his mom. She appeared to be the most excited of them all. She had invited some of the extended family members just to surprise her dear son. She had also secretly rehearsed what to say about Marvin as soon as the informal career kick-off celebration got underway. *How close are you?* His mom asked.

Pretty close. Maybe twenty minutes or less, Marvin responded, making a conscious effort to satisfy his mom's curiosity.

Just then, Marvin ran the red light. Obviously, it was not intentional, as he wasn't paying attention. He got carried away by the telephone conversation with his mom. It could have resulted in a fatal T-bone accident. Fortunately, there were no cars coming from the other direction of the road. Funnily enough, he didn't even realize he ran red lights as he drove on, keeping his mom abreast of his current location.

Unfortunately, there was a police vehicle right there at the intersection. It was Brett's official patrol vehicle. He watched as Marvin ran the red lights and never bothered to slow down. So he chased after Marvin and pulled him over. As soon as Marvin spotted the lights from Brett's patrol vehicle behind him from the mirror, he pulled up on the shoulder. *I'll call you right back,* he promised his mom, as he hung up and placed his phone on his lap.

What the heck is going on? He wondered as he watched Brett step out of his patrol car. It took Marvin a split second to switch from wondering to anger as soon as he discovered the officer who stepped out of the patrol car had a racial identity portrayed to him and his siblings by their dad as being devilish—a race whose people should be viewed as enemies and adversaries. This had always been Marvin's opinion. He left home but the first lesson he had listened to from dad several years ago never left him.

As Brett got closer, Marvin's anger did not only grow some more, it actually got fiercer. *Why did he pull me over? What did he pull me over for?* He asked himself endlessly as he impatiently watched Brett walk towards him. For Marvin, it was the longest forty-five second walk he had ever seen as he couldn't wait to unravel the mystery behind his being pulled over.

Finally, Brett caught up with him. As soon as he saw Marvin, he discovered Marvin had a racial identity he had formed an opinion about when he was living with his parents. Suddenly, he remembered one of the life lessons from his dad. Strange enough, he always did whenever he comes in close contact with people of this specific race. People of this race were a societal menace whose favorite pastime is fomenting trouble and committing crime, he would quote his dad verbatim.

With this statement in his mind, Brett switched to his usual stereotype mode. He concluded in his mind that Marvin's unintentional action of traffic violation was a deliberate attempt to live up to the societal menace misnomer. In other words, he already pre-judged Marvin based on his racial identity.

Expectedly, Brett and Marvin's meeting in this circumstance was not a pleasant one to say the least. Marvin already saw Brett as a foe based on pre-judgement, and Brett was already stereotypical even before he asked Marvin any question. To Brett, Marvin was either high on drugs or had some drugs in the car that he needed to promptly get to his patrons. Evidently there are just two things that happen when two people see each other as enemies: They switch to either an attack or a defense mode.

Do you realize you just ran red lights and almost killed two families at the intersection? Brett exaggerated.

Marvin was still angry and never said a word. He felt it was an insult to respond to a perceived enemy who was all out to attack him. At this time, Brett had also felt insulted that Marvin did not provide him any response.

Infuriated, Brett began to yell orders at Marvin. *Can I see your driver's license?*

Why would you want to see my driver's license? Marvin queried.

You need to cut it off right now, Brett warned. *I need you to produce your driver's license,* he requested again. It became obvious that Marvin would not have any of that, as he did not make any attempt to reach for his driver's license, let alone produce it.

Brett became more furious and ordered Marvin to step out of the car. After yelling the *Step out of the car* order several times with Marvin making no attempt to step out of the car, Brett reached for the door handle on Marvin's car in an attempt to force it open. Marvin held on firmly from the other side of the door. Brett struggled with the door from the outside and applied more pressure and force. Brett panted uncontrollably as he eventually overpowered Marvin. Out of provocation, he flung the door open and literally dragged Marvin out of the car.

As soon as Marvin was dragged out of the car, several bouts of altercation ensued. While some motorists pulled up to see how they could possibly be of help, a good number of them just brought out their cell phones to record the now-wild altercation. In no time, punches began to fly from both directions. The tight fists of both men became launch stations of a sort. Their jaws, noses and lips were not spared as the punches landed precisely at the right targets on their faces.

At this point, Brett realized he would not be able to bring Marvin to a reasonable submission. He attempted to reach his radio for a backup call. Just then, Marvin saw Brett's divided attention as an opportunity to win the fight. He moved swiftly towards Brett in an attempt to grab his left foot and slam him on the ground.

Unfortunately, Brett thought he wanted to reach for his gun. Brett grabbed the gun before Marvin could reach for his foot, and within a split second opened fire on Marvin three times.

Like a park of cards, Marvin wobbled from his knee joints. His skin was no match for the bullets as they pierced through his body. He felt as if some of his internal organs tore apart. His taste buds sent a salty sensation down his throat. His irresistible sonorous sweet voice that was once a prospective assurance of success could only emit sounds of excruciating pain.

He attempted to beckon folks who were standing by for help, but the strength needed to do that failed. He was only able to see split images of everyone. At this moment, the only cognitive function his mind could engage in was the sudden realization of the fact that the punctured veins were already sprinkling blood on all of his internal organs—evidence of excessive damage to some vital internal organs.

He could only watch, very faintly, as the earth rotated underneath his feet. As the clock ticked, he lost consciousness some more. Within seconds, his feet gave way as they could no longer hold his body weight—the same weight they had conveniently and comfortably carried all his life. He collapsed, landing on his face right on the asphalt.

The first set of backup responders arrived and called for an ambulance. The paramedics arrived in no time, swinging into action to see if Marvin could be revived. Without flipping him over, they lifted him on the stretcher and wheeled him into the ambulance. Professionally, the paramedics tried all they could. They administered cardiopulmonary resuscitation on him with intermittent chest compression as the ambulance raced towards the local hospital. At the ER, the doctors on duty took over from the paramedic team.

Unfortunately and regrettably, it was too late. Marvin died. He had died right inside the ambulance on the way to the hospital. The doctors realized that as soon as they took over from the paramedic team. His body was labeled dead on arrival afterwards.

It was one death too many. First and foremost, considering the magnitude of the excruciating pains he had to deal with in the last couple of minutes of his life. Secondly, considering the tragic end of his aspirations, especially as he got so close to actualizing the dreams he tirelessly worked for all his life as well as the short-lived hopes of his parents.

Notes from Illogical Reasoning: Mental Indolence Scenario

For Both Brett and Marvin

- Brett and Marvin have different racial identities.
- They do not have mutual respect for each other.
- They both have stereotypical beliefs.

For Brett

- A poor display of professionalism.
- He prejudged Marvin based on his race.

- He made an erroneous assumption that Marvin's action must have been triggered by excessive drug intake.

- His actions throughout the encounter show that he does not treat people as individuals but according to their race.

For Marvin

- He assumed that he was pulled over based on his race.

- He viewed Brett as an individual of a certain race and not as a law-enforcement agent.

- He had an erroneous belief that Brett was an enemy based on his race.

- He did not follow Brett's orders.

The Outcome

- There was a heated altercation.

- There was an unnecessary display of ego.

- An encounter that could have ended up in a warning or citation for traffic violation, ended up being a terrible situation.

- There was a senseless loss of life.

- There was a possible outbreak of chaotic demonstrations.

CHAPTER 5:

THE ROOTS

A human being is a part of the whole called by us universe,
a part limited in time and space.

– Albert Einstein

I am, by nature, an optimistic individual with a strong any-thing-can-happen mentality. I always see a solution to any issue no matter how daunting or challenging. However, having personally studied the human race alongside its behavioral pattern and peculiarities for several years, it does not seem like the long trail of racism will reach a dead end anytime soon.

There is no amount of strategy, procedure, policy or legislation that could possibly eradicate racism in its entirety. Neither will a rally, protest, seminar, symposium or a well-orchestrated orientation proffer a lasting solution to the scourge of hatred bred by racism.

No! None of these will ever hunt racism to extinction. One of the reasons is that some people are just simply who they are—rigid, proud, egocentric (self-centered, self-conscious, self-righteous), heart-less, annoyingly argumentative (the "always right" mentality), not open to dialogue (peace), not open to change, hateful, unforgiving and narrow-minded.

The love of money is the root of all evil (I Timothy 6:10). Evidently, this is one of the most popular statements in the Bible. It is imperative to note that the Holy Bible did not specifically attribute evil to money but to the love of it. Maybe most evils in our world would decline or be totally eradicated if people did not love and worship money the way they do. In the same vein, maybe if some people just genuinely took a time out and thought deeply about the roots of racism, our world could be cured of the scourge.

Rigidity

Every human, race notwithstanding, has a belief system that he or she is plugged into. For the most part, these belief systems are direct offshoots of certain agents of social change like family, school, religion (church, mosque, temple), and political affiliation. The list is inexhaustible.

These are all very strong agents of social change that form the pivot upon which our belief systems swing. Specifically, family appears to be the strongest of them all. The reason is not unconnected to the fact that from baby to infancy, and adolescence to young adulthood, humans' first point of contact is the family.

Until humans start thinking for themselves, they tend to believe whatever they are fed by their parents or guardians in term of information. These pieces of information could either be historical or twisted history, facts or made-up facts (which are no longer facts anyway), training, upbringing and so on.

While socializing with family at a very tender age, some kids are unfortunately fed the wrong information and consciously or unconsciously imbibe the spirit of animosity towards certain races other than theirs. Based on the fact that their ability to process information is not fully developed at a young age, they tend to act on impulse in connection to the information made available to them.

Unfortunately, some humans are solidly rigid by nature, and when some of these people become adults, they still wrap their arms around those pieces of wrong information they were fed as young adults because of their inability to think for themselves. These are the folks who have enormous hatred for people outside of their own race. They tend to judge people based on race rather than the content of their character.

Pride

Pride is not necessarily an unpleasant attribute. It all depends on the context. Pride is known to possess both positive and negative con-notations. A pride in the perspective of achieving a set goal allows an individual to derive an absolute satisfaction and admiration in what he or she has been able to achieve.

For instance, when a parent says to a child, *I am proud of you,* this is an expression of satisfaction or admiration of the child's achievements or behavior. So, pride in this context is utilized in a positive manner.

However, a negative pride is totally different. This makes an individual foolishly assess his or her personal values or status and place such values or status above everyone else. In the context of race, people with the propensity of negative pride, assess and evaluate their race and come up with a self-gratifying result of superiority over every other race. This is the type of pride condemned in Proverbs 16:18: *Pride goes before destruction, a haughty spirit before a fall.*

Egocentrism

The "me" attitude or mentality is the bane of any human organization anywhere in the world. Selfish people do not only think about themselves alone, they share a common notion that the entire world revolves around them. For this singular reason, other people's feelings do not, in any way, matter.

Evidently, people who care less about other races outside of their race all possess the trait of selfishness, as they tend to be self-centered, self-righteous, self-conscious, self-seeking, self-absorbed, self-important, self-interested and narcissistic.

Heartlessness

This can best be described as the inability to show a genuine concern for others. People who imbibe this trait are generally not compassionate. The power of empathy is an effective tool utilized by sales professionals. This tool is deployed whenever a prospect's or a customer's unpleasant feelings are detected, and then the sales professional instantly identifies with such prospect or customer in those moments of unpleasant feelings of fear of making a purchase decision or expression of dissatisfaction over a purchased product or service.

In this situation, a display of empathy on the part of the sales professional places the prospect on a comfortable platform, having realized that the salesperson identifies with his or her plight. In the same vein, someone with a good heart does not create an imaginary borderline on the subject of race. A good heart lets you deal with people across the board in the same way and not according to their race.

Heartless folks are more likely to be racists. This set of people do not have an iota of empathy in them. They take joy in the plight of others and are not moved by the situation of people around them or far from them. It is pretty easy for people in this category to be hostile towards people, most especially people outside of their race.

Argument

Argument ensues when an ordinary exchange of views, especially opposing views, becomes heated and eventually laced with anger. For those who have to deal with people every day at the workplace, you will realize the fact that some folks are just extremely argumentative. It really does not matter if they are right or wrong. They easily get offended whenever someone holds a contrary view to theirs.

This becomes a great deal of concern when someone with a tendency of racism possesses an argumentative trait. The point he raises and maintains all the time is that every other race is inferior to his race. He argues this whenever the slightest opportunity to do so presents itself. No one could possibly articulate any point otherwise. To him, whoever does so automatically becomes a contender or a sworn enemy. In all sanity, describing people in superlatives should be based on their character individually and not specifically about race collectively.

People with an argumentative mindset never take time off to realize that the world is not about how well you project or elevate your race, but how well you project, elevate and promote love that in turn ensures a peaceful coexistence of all races.

Dialogue

This is similar to the people discussed under "Argument," above. The only difference is that the set of people in this category are not open to dialogue at all. In other words, they won't even create a forum where an exchange of ideas could possibly take place—a forum where conversation could lead to an argument, an argument to a disagreement, and a disagreement to an agreement. Instead, the attitude here is, *My race is the most superior. Period. No controversy. I really do not want to talk to anyone (outside of my race). Period!*

Dialogue is one powerful and effective tool capable of brokering a peace treaty between people who have found themselves on opposite sides of a fence. Regrettably, this same tool can be incapacitated when people on opposite sides of a fence swear never to have anything to do with this powerful tool.

Change

It is often said that the only thing that is permanent in this world is change. Change, as a permanent occurrence, has the ability to influence a rigid stance. However, on the subject of racism, some die-hard racists are not open to change. As a result of this, it is extremely difficult to sway these people from the opinion they have long held from their formative years under their parents when they were given a totally wrong orientation about races outside of their race.

People in this category tend to experience maturity exclusively in physical body growth—height, weight, facial structure and so on. Sadly, they never experienced maturity intellectually as they intuitively act or reason based on what they've been fed with at the time they couldn't think for themselves.

Unfortunately, people in this category, for the rest of their lives, won't change their wrong perception of other races borne out of hatred and fired-up animosity simply because they lack the ability to reason that people should be evaluated based on their individual traits and characteristics rather than race.

Hatred

The word "hatred" expresses a very strong feeling of an immeasurable depth of emotional dislike. This heinous feeling, for the most part, operates on a brutal level when it is directed towards people of other races. The results have always been bias, discrimination and ultimately murder. Yes! People kill people as a result of hatred bred by racism.

I remember growing up under my parents. I have three sisters and one brother. As kids, one of the words we dared not use inside and outside of the house was "hate." For instance, you could not say you hate people based on how they look, where they live, their religion, their belief, their social status, their personality, their tribe, their ethnic group or their race.

As a matter of fact, we couldn't say *I hate you* or *I hate so and so*. Simply put, we just couldn't say *I hate*. Any time you made that statement as a kid, either by mistake or whatever your reason was, my mom would make sure you remembered the punishment after giving you a smack on the mouth from where those words she detested so much came from.

Being a devout Christian, she would make statements like *The only thing you are allowed to hate is sin, but not a sinner. You cannot hate fellow human beings like you, no matter who they are or where they are from.* With this kind of upbringing, all five of us kids learnt how not to hate people based on their race, tribe, religion or social status.

Forgiveness

Believe it or not, inability to forgive may be connected to the reason some folks end up being racists. Historically, members of certain races just ruminate on what members of a specific race did to their forefathers in term of injustice or inhumane treatments decades and centuries ago as documented in the annals of history. For this reason, they just develop strong animosity towards such a race each time and every time it crosses their mind, even though the main perpetuators of the so-called injustice no longer exist on the surface of the earth.

Isn't it time to detach ourselves from the past and live our lives to the fullest, loving everyone? The past is for history, the present is for us and the future is for God.

The forefathers of members of a certain race may have committed strings of atrocities. But why should the descendants of such forefathers suffer for the crimes they didn't commit directly? We all make mistakes, and I'm still waiting to hear from any individual or group of people with the audacity to claim they have never made a mistake.

As a matter of fact, great men and women in history wrap their arms around mistakes, define what mistakes are and how best to turn them into strength rather than tools of division. Here are some examples.

Vincent Van Gogh

Even the knowledge of my own fallibility cannot keep me from making mistakes. Only when I fall do I get up again.

John Powell

The only real mistake is the one from which we learn nothing.

Mark Twain

Forgiveness is the fragrance the violet sheds on the heel that has crushed it.

Alexander McQueen

You can only go forward by making mistakes.

Edmund Burke

Nobody made a greater mistake than he who did nothing because he could do only a little.

These are just a few great people who understand that it's okay for humans as mere mortals to make mistakes. We just need to learn from these mistakes, forgive whole-heartedly and move on.

It is appalling to realize the fact that some people have taken an unforgiving spirit to a whole new level. A few years ago in my MBA class, one of our professors who facilitated *Applied Business Research and Statistics* shared with us a story of how his marriage to his wife was almost deterred due to the weird, unforgiving spirit of her dad.

His potential father-in-law at the time he was dating his daughter was strongly against their union. They are all of the same race. The crime of my professor at the time, according to him, was that he owned and drove a BMW. This potential father-in-law would angrily warn his daughter against a relationship with my professor. *Why would an American drive a German car? Has he forgotten all the havoc wreaked by Adolf Hitler around the world during World War II? Why would he patronize a German auto company?*

In other words, this potential father-in-law still carried a considerable level of bitterness from several decades ago. As a result, he really did not want to have anything to do with not only the Germans but anything that emanated from them and by extension anyone who used German products.

Instead of throwing his arms around a responsible, well-behaved and well-mannered suitor of his daughter, he looked away from the content of the young man's character and focused his mind on an ignoble stereotype. To him, anyone who uses German products must be a narcissist and an unpatriotic American, and as such should be discriminated against. Personally, I see this as the most heinous display of an unforgiving spirit.

Believe it or not, there are several thousands of people like him. They just don't want to see and treat human beings based on who they are individually. They would rather treat people based on prejudice.

Narrow-mindedness

One of the qualities associated with great people around the globe is the size of their minds. Most great people think out of the box. The broadness of their minds always creates and sets new courses for humanity. A narrow-minded person sees, treats, and relates with people based on their race; but someone with a broad mind sees, treats, and relates with people based on who they are character-wise.

A narrow-minded individual is intellectually disabled. He finds it extremely difficult to think outside the box, so he tends to believe every bit of unsubstantiated information he was given by different misguided agents of socialization in those formative years as a kid or young adult.

Unfortunately, he becomes erratic in his dealings with people outside of his race for the rest of his life, since he is intellectually imma- ture and lacks the ability to dissociate himself from the bandwagon of people who act intuitively based on stereotype.

It is imperative to note that a misguided agent of socialization teaches avoidance based on race; but a well-guided agent of social- ization teaches avoidance based on character content.

However, it is a different ballgame for the broad-minded. People in this category are intellectually strong and active. They meticulously evaluate every bit of unsubstantiated information they were fed with at the time they didn't have minds of their own. They conduct their own research when they become adults. They filter through pieces of information, discard misguided information based on sentiments, and hold on to facts that are devoid of falsification. These are the everyday folks who treat people across all platforms of race the same way.

CHAPTER 6:
RACE CHOICE

All I ever wanted was to reach out and touch another
human being not just with my hands but with my heart.
– Tahereh Mafi.

In life, choice is about making a decision. A decision can only be made when faced with a variety of possibilities. A specific possibility decided upon is absolutely an individual's choice. Therefore, it isn't out of place to say an individual has an absolute control over choice but not necessarily over the attendant repercussions of a choice made. With every choice comes an aftermath or a list of results of the choice made. See this as a coin with two sides: choice on one side and choice outcome on the other.

On the choice side, an individual is extremely powerful. On this side, the pendulum could be wielded to oscillate in the direction that pleases the individual. Here, control and direction are simply the prerogative of the individual. However, it's a different ballgame on the other side. Once an individual is done wielding all the infinitive influences on the choice side of the coin, he or she eventually makes a choice and immediately crosses over to the choice-outcome side.

On this side, the extreme power, like a spluttering sound, fizzles. The influence also disappears, with reality taking up the role of control. It is on the choice-outcome side that an individual relinquishes the driver's seat and the inevitable aftermath of the choice made on the choice side takes over the driver's seat. An individual can only watch as choice aftermath steers the wheel at will.

With the loss of control, an individual is stuck with whatever life throws at him on the choice-outcome side. The most worrisome concern is that there isn't anything one can do to stop what life throws at one on this side. The best thing you can possibly do is to come up with strategies to adequately and effectively manage whatever life now throws at you. Evidently, this is the reality of dichotomy of choice: an opportunity to make a choice and the inevitability of the outcome of the choice made.

However, if you can't deal with the road bumps of your choice, you'll have to patiently go through a process that'll take you back to the choice side of the coin and utilize your control all over again to make another choice from the list of available possibilities. Again, be prepared for new set of attendant challenges of your new choice when you cross over to the choice-outcome side.

With this in mind, an individual could make a choice of a specific career, religion, political affiliation, husband, wife or could decide to be single. You have all the control and power to make all of these choices on the choice side of the coin. For instance, once you make a choice of a religion through your power of choice, you have no control over the tenets of that religion. You'll have to deal with those tenets at the choice-outcome side. Once you chose a career, be ready to deal with the occupational hazards specific to that career.

In the same vein, once you chose a husband or a wife out of several billion people in the world, be ready to deal with your chosen partner's attitude, either pleasant or unpleasant. It might be too harsh to say you deserve it, since you chose your partner willingly utilizing your power of choice. But then, that's the inevitable result of a choice—the reality of life.

Unfortunately, there are some limitations to this analogy of choice and choice-outcome dichotomy. With all the unbelievably immense powers and influences every individual possesses on the choice side, there isn't anyone who could possibly use the choice power to decide his or her own race. No one can make a choice of race. Absolutely none.

When it comes to people of other races, all the intelligent people I've had an opportunity to meet seem to always think right and alike. Most especially, those who understand the concepts of exception and limitation to the power of decision-making on the choice side. They have always posited that *They can possibly be us and we can as well be them. I can possibly be them and they can as well be me.* The question is this. Generally, if people on earth lack the ability to decide their own race, what is the logic behind discriminating against people based on their race? It doesn't look like there is a logical reasoning or moral justification for it. Arguably, the only set of people who can engage anyone along the line of logical reasoning as the basis for justifying their ignoble stance on race-inclined discrimination would be those who, through their absolute possession of power on choice side, decided their own race. But since there are no folks in this category, then the fact that "you can possibly be them and they can as well be you" sounds more like it is indisputable.

The fact that victims of race-inclined discrimination exist beats my imagination. This will also beat the imagination of any rational-thinking human being. Why would anyone face challenges on the choice-outcome side when he or she did not make a race choice on the choice side?

As adults, there is only so much we can remember about those days of infancy. No matter how smart you are, or how retentive your memory is, you surely can't remember your first day—the moment you were born. That moment your mother had you skips everyone's memory.

At some point in life, we just realize we are here. And as time progresses, we begin to do what other people do. At different stages of life, we begin to feel what other people feel, too: breathe, eat, drink, play, focus, study, laugh, cry, get excited, be dejected, be hopeful or hopeless, prepare or be undecided, take a step, make a move, retreat, lose focus, retrace steps, make mistakes, make amends, go astray, find a turning point, make choices (wrong or right), succeed, fail, sleep, wake and eventually die someday, somehow, somewhere.

So, is anyone really born guilty of a crime? Did anyone really have an opportunity to decide his or her own race? Sometimes, you may find an answer right inside a question. A whole lot of meditation or healthy debate could possibly change the way we think or sway an age-long opinion.

How did we get here? How possible is it to talk about race and not talk about creation? How did the human race start? There has been a wide range of accounts and propounded theories ascribed to how the human race began. An attempt to go in-depth into every belief system might deviate a little from the main purpose of this book.

However, it will be a lot helpful to scratch the surface just so a decision can be reached on whether some folks are born criminals based on their race. In addition, maybe some folks are so fortunate as to have the opportunity to pre-decide exactly what race they would be on their way here.

When it comes to the human race and its roots, there have been lots of developed belief systems over the centuries, with each providing its own argument in support of claims on how humans came into existence.

Creationism

This belief system holds an assertion of a supreme God with a supreme power who created the universe through divinity. Generally, this belief system is central to Christianity, Islam and Judaism. Maimonides, the renowned Medieval Jewish philosopher, opined that this is the only concept that applies to all three of these religions.

Specifically for Christians, this belief system is, to a large extent, connected to the assertion from the book of Genesis in the Holy Bible of how God created:

- Heaven and Earth.
- Light.
- Firmament.
- Gathered water in one place (seas).
- Dry land (Earth).
- Grass.
- Herb-yielding seeds.
- Fruit-tree yielding fruit.
- Division of day and night (for signs, seasons, days, years, Earth illumination).

- Two great lights—greater lights to rule the day and lesser light to rule the night.

- Stars (to rule over the day and night).

- Aquatic creatures.

- Birds to fly in the open firmament of heaven with a divine order/instruction to multiply.

- Then, he created living creatures—cattle and creeping things as well as beasts of the earth.

According to the book of Genesis in the Holy Bible, after creating everything in the order enumerated above, God then created humans (male and female) in his own image and gave them dominion over all his creatures. It is imperative to note that humans were created in his own image with no emphasis on race.

Genesis 1:28-31:

28 And God blessed them, and God said unto them, be fruitful, and multiply, and replenish the earth, and subdue it: and have dominion over the fish of the sea, and over the fowl of the air, and over every living thing that moves upon the earth.

29 And God said, Behold, I have given you every herb-bearing seed, which is upon the face of all the earth, and every tree, in which is the fruit of a tree yielding seed; to you it shall be for meat.

30 And to every beast of the earth, and to every fowl of the air, and to everything that crepes upon the earth, wherein there is life, I have given every green herb for meat: and it was so.

31 And God saw everything that he had made, and, behold, it was very good. And the evening and the morning were the sixth day."

Again, it is also imperative to take note of the emphasis on all God's creatures as being good. God, the creator, must have foreseen a possibility of an outbreak of race superiority war among the human race. This assertion may have as well explained why some biblical passages specifically instructed that we love our neighbors as ourselves. Such references include:

Leviticus 19:18	Luke 6:36	I John 4:7
Job 6:14	John 13:14	II Peter 1:5-7
Ecclesiastes 4:4	John 13:34	I Thes. 3:12
Isaiah 1:17	I Peter 3:8	I Thes. 5:11
Isaiah 58:6	I Peter 4:8	I Cor. 10:24
Matthew 7:12	I John 3:11	Galatians 5:14
Matthew 18:21	I John 3:16	Galatians 6:2
Mark 12:30 -31	I John 3:17	Galatians 6:10
Philippians 2:3	Romans 13:10	Romans 15:7
Hebrews 13:1-2	Romans 14:5	Colossians 3:13
Romans 2:1	Romans 14:13	James 1:27
Romans 12:10	Romans 15:2	Zech. 7:9-10
Romans 13:9	Romans 15:7	Galatians 3:28

Over the years, the evolutionists have always referred to creationism as pseudoscience. They are of the opinion that it does not in any way conform to the set methodology synonymous with science in general and specific branches of science that touch on how humans came into existence. These specific branches of science include but are not limited to Life Sciences, Astronomical Sciences, Physical Sciences and Earth Sciences.

Some evolutionists have also referred to creationism as cosmogonic myth, which merely gives a narrative account of the beginning of the world and how humans came into existence in a "fanciful" manner. While some of these evolutionists believe there are fragments of truth in what they refer to as creation myth, a considerable number of them are still of the opinion that all postulations that are myth-inclined do not only have sacred accounts that share the features of pseudoscience but the accounts are also etiological. Hence their deep level of unacceptance.

In addition, it is important to note that Creationism has also evolved into **Old Earth Creationists** and **Young Earth Creationists** over the years.

- Old Earth Creationists wrap their arms around deep time. They tend to share a notion held by natural researchers dating back to the early part of the nineteenth century with a claim that this Earth we live on has existed for billions of years, as against an assertion by Young Earth Creationist that the earth has just been in existence for a few thousand years.

- Young Earth Creationists, on the other hand, align their belief system with the Holy Bible's historical antecedent of the beginning of the human race (as accounted for in the book of Genesis). This sect is known to always reject evolution.

Evolutionism

This sect's ideology is deeply rooted in earth, physical, life and astronomical sciences. It is, to a large extent, scientists' extended investigation of cosmology in line with a strict adherence to the concept of rationality and empiricism.

The history of the Earth plays a consequential role in this belief system, as reference is often made to how living organisms metamorphosed from their earlier forms. So, to this sect, there is a strong propensity that everything has a natural ability within itself to develop into its own form (biological evolution). As a social theory, this belief system has a considerable level of influence on anthropological and sociological reasoning (at least before the First World War). Evolutionism also postulates that there is a systematic development from simpler to more complex organizational forms.

However, in the nineteenth century, series of comparative projects were attempted. These comparative projects have served as yardsticks with which subsequent comparative studies in anthropology are measured. Specifically, a cross-cultural comparison reveals a finding that is christened "the psychic unity of mankind"—some form of confirmation of racial homogeneity of mankind as against a crusade of heterogeneity of mankind capable of spreading hate.

Like creationism with **Old Earth Creationist** and **Young Earth Creationist** versions, evolutionism also has versions, known as Atheistic/Agnostic Evolutionists and Theistic Evolutionists.

- Atheistic/Agnostic Evolutionists
  These are evolutionists who believe evolution is without God.

- Theistic Evolutionists.
  These are evolutionists who believe evolution is with God.

However, whatever an individual belief system is, either as a creationist or evolutionist, the fact that applies across board is that we all found ourselves here at some point. There hasn't been any propounded theory that has convincingly postulated that humans have the ability to decide their own races prior to birth.

Whoever or whatever we turn out to be in term of race is not unconnected with heredity, genes transferred to an individual from the biological parents. With this in mind, it won't be out of place to say the creator created race, but humans, out of hate and unhealthy rivalry, created racism.

CHAPTER 7:

WORLD VERSUS RACISM

One love, one heart, one destiny.

– Bob Marley

Arguably, racism is as old as the world itself. It sure has a hate undertone. Hate is bred by jealousy, envy or just a bizarre feeling of hatred towards a particular race or specific races. If syllogism is anything to go by, one could posit that: All racists are haters of specific races, Mr. Whoever hates members of specific races, and therefore, Mr. Whoever is a racist.

In addition, while all racists might be classified as haters in the context of race, not all haters, in general terms, are racists. As discussed earlier, jealousy and envy could trigger hatred but may not necessarily trigger racism.

The first murder case recorded in the Holy Bible was the murder crime perpetuated by Cain against his brother, Abel. Cain developed a great deal of hatred for Abel borne out of jealousy and envy. He had an ignoble opinion that Abel was his parents' and God's favorite based on rejection and acceptance of offer of sacrifice. He failed to study what constituted good and acceptable sacrifice.

Instead, he channeled the amount of energy required to fine-tune his offer of sacrifice (and elevate it into an acceptable status) to developing enormous hatred for Abel—a wrongly channeled energy that eventually led to him killing his brother.

The biblical account of this murder case was simply an action taken based solely on envy. It does not, in any way, qualify to be treated as an action propelled by racism, as they were siblings from the same biological parents and as such members of the same race. In other words, while racism could be hate-inclined, hate might not necessarily be race-inclined.

Evidently, from the inception of the world, hatred has been a major menace. Aside the hate story of Cain and Abel, one of the first accounts of racism is reflected in the story of Moses. Events that unfolded around him from birth seemed to have all unfolded in his favor. He was a Jew who grew up in the splendor, opulence and grandeur of royalty in and around pharaoh's palace. He was shielded from hate, slavery and possible discrimination by pharaoh's daughter's love.

Moses probably saw the excruciating pains of slavery through exhausting labor and freedom restriction that characterized everyday living for his people. He probably knew what discrimination smelled like from a distance and at a close range, but he never experienced it first-hand.

Moses' first-hand experience with racism was documented in Numbers Chapter 12. Moses, a Jew, had gone outside of his race to marry a Cushite woman. The Jews are the direct descendants of Jacob, the patriarch and grandson of father Abraham. History has it that after the Exodus (the departure of the people of Israel from Egypt c. 1300 BC), they established the kingdoms of Israel and Judah.

Kingdom of Kush, on the other hand, happened to be an ancient kingdom in Nubia—a section/region located along river Nile (between Aswan, south Egypt and Khartoum, central Sudan). This kingdom prides itself as one of the foremost centers of early civilization in ancient Africa.

Obviously, there was a skin color difference, which noticeably denoted that they are both members of different races. On meeting Moses' wife, there was an instant disapproval by Miriam, Moses' sister, as well as Aaron. Moses' wife's only crime was being a Cushite.

By Miriam's standard, the Cushite lady was born a criminal. She was not of Hebrew origin and therefore was not good enough for her brother. Remember how God, in Genesis 1:28-31, referred to everything he had created as being good? Miriam's position on the Cushite lady seemed to have been at variance with God's position on his creatures, and her racist stance and comments earned her an instant judgement.

From Ancient History (60,000 BC – 650 AD) to the Postclassical Era (500 – 1500), Modern History (1500 – present), Early Modern History (1500 – 1750), the Mid-Modern Period (1750 – 1914) to the Contemporary Period (1914 – present), there have always been wars, arguments, talks, opinions and movements based on racial supremacy.

The twentieth century cannot be dissociated from this racial supremacy chaos. It is evident that the Nazi movement was race-propelled. According to William Edward Burghardt Du Bois, a civil rights activist, educator, leader, sociologist, historian, poet, writer, editor, Pan-Africanist and scholar who was popularly known as W.E.B. Du Bois, *The problem of the twentieth century is the problem of the color line*.

Historically, many nations across the globe had, at some point in time, institutionalized segregation either by intent or by accident.

It was not only ideal to engage in dastardly acts that promoted seg-regation, slavery and racism, it was also a dangerous move to stage a crusade against it.

In the United States of America, specifically in the St Louis, Missouri area. Being specific about this area is not an attempt to insin-uate that it had the worst-case scenario. I picked on the area because I currently live there and it is a lot easier for one to research one's immediate environment.

In 1847, folks who were pro-slavery obviously supported the ban on educating people of a specific race. Earlier, in 1836, Francis L. McIntosh, a free mulatto boatman, was burned alive. The excru-ciating pain preceding his death is better left to the imagination. The crime he committed was speaking against the heinous crime of hate and segregation.

In the same manner, Elijah Lovejoy, an editor of a Presbyterian Newspaper christened the *St. Louis Observer*, who had moved to the St Louis, Missouri area in June 1833, found himself in the middle of an ugly mess because of his series of editorials that strongly expressed intolerance for segregation, slavery and racism.

After a series of attempts on his life as well as several attacks on the newspaper's office, Lovejoy decided to relocate to Alton, Illinois where slavery was an illegal practice sequel to the Northwest Ordinance of 1787. The ordinance, adopted by the Second Continental Congress, made provision for government of the Northwest Territory and also put in place a method for incorporating new states into the Union from the territory. In addition to this, the ordinance also established a list that contains a bill of rights guaranteed in the territory. Interestingly, one of the main provisions of the ordinance was the fact that it out-rightly outlawed slavery.

One can only imagine the breath of fresh air felt by Lovejoy having moved to Alton. He had thought he was free from those damaging criticisms of his well-articulated editorials committed to justice, fairness and the course of humanity. He settled down at his newly found abode of peace—or so he thought.

He swung into action afterwards, publishing articles geared towards breaking the backbone of hate and segregation. Unfortunately, he was wrong in thinking he had found a safe haven, as he was attacked and brutally murdered later that year by a misguided pro-slavery mob. Lovejoy paid the ultimate price, his dear life, for a course he believed in.

If there was anyone who would connect with Lovejoy, it would be Frances Dana Gage. She, like Lovejoy, had moved to the St Louis, Missouri area from Ohio around 1853. She had presided over the National Women's Rights Convention in Cleveland. In the 1840s and 1850s, she focused on feminism and wrote in-depth articles for both regional and national newspapers. For some reason, Gage switched priorities. She suddenly became passionate about the plight of victims of segregation, hate and slavery. In a quick succession, she hopped from the platform of feminism to that of abolition.

For Gage, her new passion was a leap of courage, knowing fully well the several bouts of resistance she would have to contend with. She evaluated her level of resilience and concluded in her mind that she was ready for the imminent battle ahead.

She directed all her energies and writing skills towards freedom for victims of segregation and slavery. The authorities later started killing her stories by simply refusing to publish her columns that were geared towards giving a voice to the voiceless. She not only suffered the attendant dejections associated with being silenced, her house was burned down several times by a group of heartless extremists.

Many nations in the contemporary world have enacted laws aimed at fighting against segregation. From the United Kingdom to Australia and from the United States to Germany, it is getting increasingly difficult to pretend it does not exist.

In the United Kingdom, *The Race Relations Act of 1965* happens to be the first-known legislation specifically promulgated to address the menace of racial discrimination. Discrimination was outlawed by this act on the grounds of national origin, race, color or ethnicity.

In the United States, there are several federal laws that specifically prohibit race-based discrimination. *The Civil Rights Act of 1964* was aimed at protecting individuals against discrimination. The act was fortified with anti-discrimination provisions, which include:

- Title I
  Addressed the unequal application of voters' registration requirements. However, issues like literacy tests (a method that was adopted in an attempt to exclude prospective voters of certain races/people of specific social status), police repression and economic retaliation were not specifically addressed.

  Though the act made provisions for equal voting procedures and rules across the board, it did not clear the air on the qualification of voters. You can simply put it this way. It cleverly postulates/supports an idea that the right to vote is way beyond citizenship, as strings like meeting some other set standard beyond citizenship were attached. Essentially, citizenship in itself did not automatically guarantee you the right to vote.

However, about a year after enacting *The Civil Rights Act of 1964*, *The Voting Rights Act of 1965* was enacted. The sole aim of the new act was to play a "cleanup" role after *The Civil Rights Act of 1964*.

The Voting Rights Act of 1965 has been referred to at different times as a "landmark piece of federal legislation" in the United States. Interestingly, the Congress had to amend the Act a total of five times to ensure its provisions and protections were more robust.

It signified the beginning of a new era as it marked the first time certain races became statutorily protected from racial discrimination in voting. It is important to note that this act, as signed into law by President Lyndon Johnson, was right at the peak of the Civil Rights Movement

The Voting Rights Act was a positive response to the clarion calls of the marginalized. The act enforced the voting rights provided for by the **Fourteenth Amendment** (adopted on July 9, 1868 to address citizenship rights as well as equal protection of the law) and the **Fifteenth Amendment** (ratified on February 3, 1870 to prohibit both federal and state governments from denying the right of a citizen to vote based on "race, color or previous condition of servitude") to the United States Constitution.

- Title II
  This title basically outlawed discrimination on the grounds of color, race, national origin, religion or race in restaurants, motels, hotels, theaters and other places considered public.

- Title III

  Prohibited all tiers of government from denying access to public facilities on the grounds of national origin, race, color or religion.

- Title IV

  Authorized the United States Attorney General to file suits to enforce desegregation of public schools.

- Title V

  Additionally fortifies the Civil Rights Commission (as established by Civil Rights Act of 1957) with more powers, rules and procedures.

- Title VI

  Government agencies that receive federal funds are prevented from discrimination by this title. Any agency that violates this title may lose federal funding. The title ensures that citizens have equal access to financial assistance programs of government.

  Section 601 stipulates that no one should be discriminated against on the grounds of race, color and national origin under any program receiving federal financial assistance.

  In other words, no one should be denied federal financial assistance benefits based on race.

  Section 602 stipulates that every federal agency that administers any program that is financial-assistance-driven, either in form of grant or loan, is authorized and directed to effectuate the provisions of section 601. Rules, regulations and orders of general applicability are not expected to be at variance with achievement of the objectives of the statute authorizing the financial assistance in connection with which the action is taken.

This section also states, in part, that all set rules, regulations and orders are subject to the President's approval before they become effective.

Section 603 states that any of the agency or department actions taken pursuant to section 602 is subject to judicial review. Personally, I guess this section further removes the possibility of prejudice in the design of the rules and regulations.

Section 604 focuses on the entire title itself, as it clearly states that "Nothing contained in this title shall be construed to authorize action under this title by any department or agency with respect to any employment practice of any employer, employment agency, or labor organization except where a primary objective of the federal financial assistance is to provide employment."

Section 605 states that nothing in the title is intended to "add to or detract from any existing authority with respect to any program or activity under which federal financial assistance is extended by way of a contract of insurance or guaranty."

- Title VII
Prohibits employers from race-based discrimination (Equal Employment Opportunity). This provision ensures that no one is discriminated against in the labor market based on race, gender, national origin, social/family status or color. It even went a step further to include people with limited proficiency in the English language.

- Title VIII
  Focuses on the voting data and compilation of voter-registration at geographic areas, as specified by Commission on Civil Rights.

- Title IX
  Proffers solution to one of the age-long complaints of the civil rights activists. This title allows for an easy move of civil rights cases to federal court from state courts. Before now, members of the civil rights community had bitterly complained of unfair trials in state courts.

- Title X
  Paves the way for the establishment of the Community Relations Service, which is saddled with the responsibility of resolving community-related disputes involving claims of discrimination.

- Title XI
  This title provides an opportunity for any defendant held in criminal contempt under titles II through VII of the Act to have a right to a jury trial. However, if convicted, such defendant can either be fined an amount not exceeding $1,000 or given a six-month prison sentence.

In the same vein, Australia wrapped its arms around protecting possible victims of racism when the nation enacted *The Racial Discrimination Act of 1975, The Human Rights and Equal Opportunity Commission Act of 1986* as well as *The Commonwealth Racial Hatred Act of 1995.* All of these have a common goal of outlawing racial discrimination.

All these promulgated acts by nations across the globe are pointers to the existence of racism as a societal menace. It also attests to the concerted efforts to rid our world of this scourge by nations who, through the enactments of these relevant laws, attempted to produce discrimination-free societies.

This has helped tremendously in protecting the interests of prospective vulnerable victims of race discrimination. In the same manner, prospective perpetuators of race-inclined hate are now compelled to act responsibly when dealing with people of different races out of fear—fear of breaking existing enacted laws.

However, the residue of several decades of institutionalized segregation and systemic racism still affects race relations till this day. This is so unfortunate.

CHAPTER 8:

THE POWER OF LOVE

I don't want to live in the kind of world where we don't look out for each other. Not just the people that are close to us, but anybody who needs a helping hand. I can't change the way anybody else thinks, or what they choose to do, but I can do my bit.

– Charles de Lint

The power inherent in love is astronomical. It is the only known weapon capable of defeating hate. Racism loses its firm grip on our world when love is applied. Everyone's involvement in the propagation of the message of love will go a long way. From presidents to the law-enforcement agents, from the sheikhs to the preachers, from the monarchs to opinion leaders—if any individual feels too insignificant to make an impact, such an individual has never been in bed with a mosquito. Despite being so insignificant in terms of size, it could give you a sleepless night—that's its own way of making an impact with its miniature size.

I remember very vividly the royal wedding between Prince Harry and Meghan Markle. I watched the live broadcast. Their marriage is very symbolic if viewed from the lens of humanity. Their union is a win for humanity: a pacesetter for a happy living, a liberation from the shackles of impossibilities. They both accepted each other the way all humans should accept one another in an ephemeral world where we are all sojourners.

The wedding surpassed everyone's expectations. Harry and Meghan were both pleasingly grand. The wedding ceremony was a perfect combination of simplicity, glamor and elegance. I paid attention to broadcasters' commentaries, evaluation and analysis of the ceremony. While some focused on the glamor, some others laid emphasis on the apparent simplicity. Yet some highlighted the outfits of the people in attendance from the queen to the guests.

For me, the main center of attraction was the sermon delivered by the Most Reverend Michael Bruce Curry, the twenty-seventh Presiding Bishop and Primate of the Episcopal Church. From the moment he mounted the stage, there was a deafening silence. Everyone could hear everyone's heartbeats. His pleasant voice broke the silence and the confidence with which he spoke restored the relaxed ambience of the ceremony.

Aside from providing a framework for Harry and Meghan where they would continue to nurture the love that binds them, Reverend Curry's message about the power of love could potentially dismantle a systemic racism and build a new world where peace and unity would reign supreme.

The Most Reverend's message was taken from the Song of Solomon 8:6-7: *Set me as a seal upon your heart. As a seal upon your arm. For love is as strong as death, jealousy as cruel as the grave. Its flashes are flashes of fire. The raging flames. Many waters cannot quench love, neither can flood drown it.*

The sermon resonated so well with me that I shed tears. As I reached out for a tissue, I also reached out for my computer at the same time. Then, I played back the sermon, and began to transcribe. After reading through the Song of Solomon passage, Most Rev. Curry quoted Dr. Martin Luther King Jr,: *We must discover the power of love. The redemptive power of love. And when we do that, we will make of this old world a new world.*

After the quotes, he dove straight into the main message of the sermon. Here is what I transcribed: *Love is the only way. There is power in love. Don't underestimate it. Don't even over-sentimentalize it. There is power...power in love. If you don't believe me, think about a time when you first fell in love. The whole world seemed to center around you and your beloved. But this power...power in love. Not just in a romantic form, but any form, any shape of love. There is a certain sense in which when you are loved, you know it. When someone cares for you and you know it. When you love and you show it. It actually feels right. There is something right about it. And there is a reason for it. The reason has to do with the source.*

Most Rev. Curry spoke with a decisive confidence and a distinctive aura. He sounded more like he has a repository of what could be best described as all about love—what love could achieve—the efficacy of the healing pattern of love—how love could change the contemporary trajectory and heal the racism-infected world completely. As everyone listened with rapt attention, the Most Reverend continued:

We were made by the power of love. And our lives are meant to be lived in that love. That's why we are here. Ultimately, the source of love is God himself. The source of all of our lives. There is no medieval pun that says where true love is found, God himself is there. The New Testament says it this way: Beloved, let us love one another because love is of God and those who love are born of God and know God. Those who do not love do not know God. Why? For God is Love.

There is power in love. There is power in love to help and heal when nothing else can. There is power in love to lift up...[and] liberate when nothing else will. There is power in love to show us the way to live. Setting as a seal on your heart. A seal on your arm. For love, it is strong as death. But love is not only about a young couple. Now the power of love is demonstrated by the fact that we are all here. Two young people fell in love and we are all filled up. But it is not just for and about a young couple who we rejoice with. It's more than that.

Jesus of Nazareth, on one occasion, was asked by a lawyer to sum up the essence of the teachings of Moses and...he went back and reached back into the Hebrews' scriptures... to Deuteronomy and Leviticus. And Jesus said, you shall love the Lord your God with all your heart, all your soul, all your mind and all your strength. This is the first and great commandment. And the second is like it, love your neighbor as yourself. And then in Mathew's version, he added and said: on these two—love of God and love of neighbor—hang all the law, all the prophets, everything that Moses wrote, everything in the holy prophets, everything in the scriptures, everything the Lord has been trying to tell the world—Love God, love your neighbors, love yourself.

Now, someone once said that Jesus began the most revolutionary movement in all of human history. A movement grounded in the unconditional love of God for the world. A movement mandating people to live, then love. And in so doing, to change not only their lives, but the very life of the world itself. I'm talking about some power. Real power. Power to change the world.

If you don't believe me, well, there were some slaves in America, who explained the dynamic power of love and why it has the power to transform. They explained it this way—they said it's spiritual, even in the midst of their captivity...it's something about a balm of Gilead—healing balm. Something that can make things right. There is a balm of Gilead to make the wounded whole. There is a balm in Gilead that heals.

If you cannot preach like Peter, and you cannot pray like Paul, you just tell the love of Jesus. How he died to save us all. Oh! That's the balm of Gilead. This way of love—it is the way of life. He died to save us all. He didn't die for anything he can get out of it. Jesus did not get an honorary doctorate for dying. He wasn't getting anything out of it. He gave up his life. He sacrificed his life for the good of others. For the good of the other. For the well-being of the world. For us. That's what love is.

Love is not selfish. Love can be sacrificial. And in so doing, becomes redemptive. And that way of unselfish, sacrificial redemptive love changes lives and it can change this world. If you don't believe me, just stop, think and imagine. Think and imagine. Well...Think and imagine a world where love is the way. Imagine our homes and families when love is the way. Imagine neighborhood and communities when love is the way. Imagine governments and Nations when love is the way. Imagine business and commerce when love is the way. Imagine this world when unselfish, sacrificial, and redemptive love is the way.

There's no child that will go to bed hungry in this world ever again. When love is the way, we will let justice roll down like a stream and righteousness like an ever-flowing river. When love is the way, poverty will become history. When love is the way, the earth will be a sanctuary. When love is the way, we will lay down our swords and shields by the riverside. There won't be war anymore. When love is the way, we will actually treat one another like...well...like we are actually family.

At this point, as soon as Most Rev. Curry made this point, I saw a very broad smile on the lips of David Beckham, the soccer legend. His smile came across more like an affirmative nod to Rev. Curry's assertion of the power of love. All through the sermon, the camera showed the faces of some of the guests. From the royal family members to the bride's mother. From Serena Williams to George Clooney. I'm not sure Rev. Curry noticed any reaction, though. He was so passionate about the sermon that it didn't appear like he noticed any reactions. So, with no particular attention to anyone specifically, he continued:

When love is the way, we know that God is the source of us all and we are brothers and sisters—children of God. My brothers and sisters, that's a new heaven, a new earth, a new world, a new human family...

Dr. King (Martin Luther King) was right. We must discover love. The redemptive power of love. And when we do that, we will make of this old world a new world. My brothers. My sisters. God loves you. God bless you. And may God hold us all in those almighty hands of love.

CHAPTER 9:

OUR WORLD

Experience, or what we call experience, is not the inventory of our pains, but rather the learned sympathy towards the pain of others.

– Juan Gabriel Vásquez

I was at home in the months that preceded the release of *I Can't breathe*, the short blockbuster movie narrated in the first chapter. It was on a Sunday evening. I had just finished watching the evening news on my favorite news channel. With nothing else on my to-do calendar for the evening, I began to prepare myself mentally for the work week ahead. I thought about the e-mails, requisitions, meetings, deadlines, projects, IMs, processes, trainings and other work-related tasks.

As I pondered over what lies ahead for the week, I made a conscious effort to let work slide off my mind while I savor the weekend rest time. The weekend would be over in just a few hours. In an undertone, I informed myself, *you'd better make good use of those hours to maximize relaxation before Monday rolls in.*

Just then, I decided to check my text messages and e-mails before committing to any other activity that qualifies for maximizing relaxation. As I flipped over to WhatsApp and tapped on the AMCOS logo to check messages on that platform, I found a video that made me ponder some more.

By the way, AMCOS is an acronym for the Association of Mass Communications Students—an association I was an integral part of back in my college days. The WhatsApp group had recently been created to provide a platform where we can all interact socially, keep in touch generally and share memories of college days.

The video was posted by one of us, Mary Omoaregba (now Mary Nwaeke). It had a total duration of three minutes and twenty-four seconds. Since I was already in relaxation mode, I excitedly pressed the play button. Instantaneously, the video responded swiftly to the play command and I watched as the timing began to count upwards.

The visual images were cosmic. The first image being that of the Earth. With a rapt interest, I watched as the camera zoomed out on the Earth image and like a deflated balloon gradually losing helium, the image became smaller and smaller.

Eventually, it transformed from small into tiny and then into a dot-like image. As I strained my eyes to make sure I didn't lose sight of the dot-like image of the Earth, it ended up strangled in the middle of scattered lights with no clear difference.

With my phone glued to my palm, I lay there and wondered how small the world we live in is. It is just an insignificant fractional part of the universe—an immeasurable space that holds our world including other known planets, stars, galaxies as well as other forms of energy and matter.

Then, I began to drift away in deep thoughts trying to make a sense of the short cosmic video I just watched. *What is in this tiny world anyway?* I queried. *Such an odd and unfair world,* I responded to my own question. A world where every stratum that represents a geographical entity has a peculiar lifestyle predetermined by culture and custom. A world where law is the only instrument that compels the majority of the people to behave rationally and conform to set standards in term of what to do and what not to do.

A world where recalcitrant folks dare to undermine the law of the land. A world where a trip to another geographical part of it presents to you several bouts of culture shock. A world where, in contemporary days, sitting or standing comfortably in a public place has been traded for mental alertness as fear of sporadic shooters is almost always present.

A world where school kids have been rudely awakened to the reality of defense and safety techniques creeping into their academic curriculum, while intermittent drills gradually take the place of physical education. A world laced with several strings of oddities.

So, what are some of these oddities? The list is simply inexhaustible. Some folks have great ideas that will transform our world in a positive manner and navigate our common ship towards a safe shore. Regrettably, many of the folks in this category do not have the power that would enable them launch or execute those great and laudable ideas. Ironically, other folks have power and do not have transformative ideas.

Some people walk or even run for miles just to burn calories as well as digest excess food intake for the day, while a whole lot of folks walk several miles to find food that will barely last them a day or take them through the night.

An odd world where two people genuinely in love never get married. A world where some folks who got married legally and genuinely are not truly in love. A world where a husband professes his love for his "dear" wife and cheats on her the next minute. A world where a wife wishes her "darling" husband dead just so she could run off with her secret lover.

A world where a husband takes an act of vice to a scary level of killing his own wife just so he could savor an ephemeral infatuation with his secret mistress.

In the same world, some folks travel to another part of the world and are referred to as expatriates, while other people travel the same way to another part of the world and are referred to as illegal immigrants.

The same world where some innocent people are arbitrarily locked up behind bars either intentionally or by mistake and criminals walk freely unchallenged on our streets. How more odd can our tiny world possibly be?

As I pondered over oddities after oddities that characterize our world, my son's call jolted me back to life. The call was received on the same phone I had watched the video on. We exchanged quick pleasantries and I went back to the AMCOS platform, which was still open anyway. Then, I looked at the time and realized how far I'd drifted into the night wondering about a three-minute, twenty-four-second video.

By now, the mental preparation for a work week ahead had been docked. Sleep had disappeared. I tossed from side to side, from one edge of the bed to the other in a manner reminiscent of restlessness.

I wanted to make more sense of the cosmic video more than anything else in the world. I wanted to ponder over more attendant odds that are associated with our world. But at this time, I could no longer think straight. Just then, I began to drift away again in deep thoughts.

If the entire unpredictable tiny world we live in is full of oddities, unfairness and so much injustice, what then is the purpose of our world? Sometimes you may find an answer in a question. Obviously, not in this one.

Like a Broadway performer receiving some kind of prompt from the director, my mind somehow got prompted by an earlier event. An event that unfolded immediately after watching the video. Then I asked myself that question once again. This time with an emphasis on the word "exactly." *What exactly is in this tiny world?*

This time, I thought very deeply about it. My mind traveled the length and breadth of some of the places in the world that I've been to: Africa, Europe, America and Arab regions. I've consciously removed "continent" from my cosmic parlance. I've not had an opportunity to visit Asia, Australia and some other regions that make up our world yet.

As my mind began to collate all the places I've visited, my senses began to build graphic visuals of these places. Within minutes, I had a complete visual image of all the places that I've ever been to. Confidently, I could beat my chest and say I know exactly what's in our world.

Unless the parts of the world I've not visited are different in term of habitation, then it won't be out of place to simply posit that everywhere is everywhere. Yes, everywhere is just simply everywhere.

Arguably, it may be right to say it's only two things that make up our world: (1) people and (2) all the other things put together. You can even go a step further to say the Earth is made up of three things: people, animals and all the other things put together.

Again, if you really want to be more elaborate, you can simply say four things: people, animals, oceans and all the other things put together. If you are meticulously analytic, you could simply say five things: people, animals, oceans, jungles and all the other things put together.

You can go on and on. You can segment the Earth based on your analytic prowess or as observed or proven by a few fields of study or related branches of science. You can also stratify the Earth based on life, habitats, territories, vegetation, seas, oceans, terrains—hills, steppe, deserts, mountains, uplands, lowlands, valleys and so on.

One thing is constant—people. We have dominion over other creatures. In an attempt to sound less complex, it may be right to simply admit that the Earth is comprised of people and all other things put together.

So, if people are the most important inhabitants of our tiny world as chief occupants, one begins to wonder why we divide ourselves along the lines of race, religion, gender, nationality, tribe and ethnicity.

Why do we add more to the odds of the world staging crusades of hate? Why, in this tiny world, do we detest one another and take joy in sowing seeds of discord? Why don't we direct our energies towards reducing the oddities that the world is already plagued with? Why is race an issue?

Have we ever focused on the blood that flows in the veins of everyone as a sign of oneness and a reason to unite? Why don't we open our eyes widely to see humanity instead of viewing humans through the lens of skin color?

As I ruminated over all of these, I realized how far into the night I'd gone. I would still need to get up early and prepare for the office. It would be Monday morning—the rush. I'm lucky, though. I really don't have to deal with the traffic jam. So, one less thing to worry about.

I work for one of the largest financial firms in the Midwest. My office is in downtown St. Louis, Missouri but I live on the Illinois side—across the river as it is fondly referred to in the St. Louis area.

I have to cross the busy Mississippi River to get to work from Monday to Friday except on the days I have to work from home. Just in case you're wondering why I don't have to contend with the traffic jam, I only drive seven minutes from home to the train station, hop on the train and let the metro service do the rest. That way, I save on gas and mileage—a rare win-win situation.

Finally, I stretched and attempted to go use the bathroom and go to bed afterwards. That was when I realized that my phone was still stuck in my palm all this while that I pondered and imagined.

I took a quick look at the phone to see if I had missed any call while I was on a trance trip with my mind behind the wheel. Then, I discovered the phone had gone into a power-saving mode. I tapped on the screen to pull it out of that mode just so I could get to my call log, but the first thing that came on was the cosmic video with the play button in the middle.

This is very normal. When your phone goes into a power-saving mode after a specific number of seconds or minutes of inactivity, the first thing you see when you try to get it out of that mode would be the last activity you were on.

For the last time, I decided to play the video again. After all, it is less than four minutes. I have no idea why I had a very strong connection with this video. Habitually, I'll watch videos posted in a group chat room or privately sent to me and delete afterwards.

It is also a habit of mine to resend some of the videos to a few folks on my contact list who I'm sure will have some kind of connection with such videos. My favorite videos are the ones that'll engage me intellectually as well as the short ones by comedians, as I love to laugh a lot.

I was glad my phone took me through the video again as I tried to navigate to my call log; otherwise, I wouldn't have thought of watching it all over again. As I tapped the play button, it rolled into play and as I reached out for pillows to raise my head in a more comfortable way, that was when I noticed something else that I didn't notice the first time I played the video. I couldn't have been more pleased with my decision to watch it all over again.

The video had been produced with a voice-over. I probably didn't notice the first time because I was too engrossed in the visuals as well as the mental interpretation I ascribed to it throughout the duration of the video.

The visual signals were so dynamic that I literally had an unexplainable connection. I was so surprised that I didn't notice the voice-over. As the voice pierced through the speaker of my phone in a flawless narrative manner, I adjusted the topmost pillow that had a direct contact with the back of my head for a more comfortable posture.

The first statement from the voice was *That's here.* At first, I didn't understand what that meant as I said to myself—*Wait a minute. What? Where?* I sounded so incoherent that I wondered if I missed any statement before that. I paused the video, leaned on the night stand, pulled the upper drawer open and reached for one of the pens arranged in an array.

CHAPTER 10:

OUR EVERYDAY WORLD

No one is born hating another person because of the color of his skin, or his background, or his religion. People must learn to hate, and if they can learn to hate, they can be taught to love, for love comes more naturally to the human heart than its opposite.

– Nelson Mandela

I have a habit of keeping pens around me all the time. The ones in the drawer of my night stand are specifically for the purpose of scribbling something of interest—anything that needs to be researched further—whenever I watch the news or any of my favorite shows.

As soon as I grabbed the pen and a writing pad, I rewound the video all the way to the beginning and tapped on the play button all over again. Then, I began to transcribe the voice-over.

Here is what I ended up transcribing:

That's here. On it, everyone you love. Everyone you know. Everyone you ever heard of, every human being who ever was, lived out their lives. The aggregate of our joy and suffering, thousands of confident religious ideologies and economic doctrines, every hunter, forager, every hero and coward.

Every creator and destroyer of civilization. Every king and peasant. Every young couple in love, every mother and father, hopeful child, inventor and explorer.

Every teacher of morals, every corrupt politician, every superstar, every supreme leader, every saint and sinner in the history of our species, lived there on a mote of dust suspended in a beam. The Earth is a very small stage in a vast, cosmic arena.

Think of the rivers of blood spilled by all those generals and emperors so that in glory and triumph, they could become the momentary masters of a fraction of a dot.

Think of the endless cruelties visited by inhabitants of one corner of the pixel on the scarcely distinguishable inhabitants of some other corner. How frequent their misunderstandings. How eager they are to kill one another. How frequent their hatreds.

Our posturing. Our imagined self-importance, the delusion that we have some privileged position in the universe, is challenged by this point of pale light.

Our planet is a lonely speck in the great, enveloping cosmic darkness. In our obscurity, in all this vastness, there is no hint that help will come from elsewhere to save us from ourselves.

The Earth is the only world known so far to harbor life. There is nowhere else, at least in the near future, to which our species could migrate.

Visit, yes. Settle, not yet. Like it or not, for the moment, the Earth is where we make our stand. It has been said that astronomy is a humbling and character-building experience. There is perhaps no better demonstration of the folly of human conceits than this distant image.

To me, it underscores our responsibility to deal more kindly with one another and to preserve and cherish the pale blue dot—the only home we've ever known.

After transcribing the voice over in the video, I read the transcribed piece over and over again. By the time I read it for the last time, I had honestly lost count of the number of times I read it. Way more than the number of times I watched the video, counting the frequency at which I paused and rewound just to be sure none of the statements slipped through the cracks.

The last statement, which simply states, *To me, it [the tiny size of the Earth] underscores our responsibility to deal more kindly with one another and to preserve and cherish the pale blue dot—the only home we've ever known,* really got me. I was sold with that last statement. I had one last read and was amazed at how well it aligned with my thought process.

I looked at the time again. *"Oh my goodness,"* I exclaimed as I realized how far into the night I had gone. I logged out of WhatsApp, slid my phone onto the charge station and like a drunk bird, staggered into the bathroom.

As soon as I was done emptying the almost-overflowing liquid in my bladder, I staggered back to the bedroom, switched off the lights, slid under the comforter and began to snore into the night.

As soon as I got up in the morning, I needed no one to tell me that I didn't have a sound sleep. My body already informed me, as it ached all over.

I was almost running late, so I hurriedly went to the bathroom, brushed my teeth, took a shower and applied some lotion. Then I flung my closet open, flipped through hung shirts, pants and ties, grabbed the ones I was able to reach first—as long as they matched—got dressed and left home sprinting like I was in a competitive race.

I'm not really huge on breakfast, so it worked out perfectly well that I gained some time skipping breakfast. This is so unlike me. I always like to take my time, as I detest rushing.

That Monday morning, as I drove towards the train station, I earnestly hoped I wouldn't fall asleep behind my desk when I get to the office. Surprisingly, I did not. I won't take the credit for that, though. It was a very busy Monday, so sleep had no chance to creep in.

At my lunchtime, I checked my personal e-mail account and went through my e-mails for the day. I replied to the ones I could and manually moved the rest into a pending folder that I created for that purpose.

As I moved the last batch, I discovered one of them was from Ameren—my power provider. I've been with Ameren since I moved to the St. Louis area from Atlanta, Georgia and I've experienced reliable service with them.

Out of curiosity, I opened the e-mail. It was a wish. Ameren had sent me a *Happy Earth Day* wish. *What is it about Earth these days?* I wondered. First, it was a previous night's Earth-related video posted by my friend Mary that got me thinking almost all night long and messed up my Monday morning. Now, it's an e-mail with content related to the same video.

Happy Earth Day? First and foremost, I never knew such a day existed. Astonishingly, Ameren's first statement in the e-mail correlated with the last statement of the voice-over in the cosmic video and aligned with my almost-all-night trance and thought process.

Like a well-orchestrated plan, Ameren had begun the e-mail message with opening information: *Earth Day is a great time to reflect on caring for our planet and the environment.* Just then, a question popped up on my mind as I started to drift away again in deep thought like I did last night.

Going by this statement by Ameren—which came across to me as being powerfully loaded—*What is in our environment?* People and all other things put together, I posited.

Maybe if we all earnestly and genuinely reflect on caring for our tiny planet and the environment and take a step forward to include people generally irrespective of skin color, nationality and race, we'll not only get rid of pollution and improve our wellness health-wise, but we'll also get rid of the negative effects of racism and help promote peace that'll make our planet a more conducive place to live in.

As I adjusted my sleeves, I suddenly remembered that I was still at the office, so I adjusted my tie and quickly snapped out of what would have been a repeat trance.

Once I confirmed that I was fully back to life, I looked at the time and realized I still had a few moments of lunch time. So I adjusted my shirt on the front side, got up from the atrium and headed towards the elevators thinking about the unfinished business of the previous night as I punched my floor number inside the elevator.

By the time I finished with the day's tasks, I had gone way beyond my regular closing time. That happens sometimes. I really don't feel it when it happens. I love my job. I love the firm I work for and the people I work with.

Just like most days, this Monday was a very good day. It was very busy, but it was exactly what I hoped for if the sleep-deprived night was anything to go by.

The train trip back to the station where I parked my car was not bad either. Once I walked back to my car, I disengaged my backpack, opened the door and flung it from the driver's side to the passenger seat. Then, I sunk myself gently on the driver's seat and drove home thinking about the incessant Earth messages and my lifelong passion of seeing a society free of racism.

Earlier in the office, I thought about the unfinished business of the previous night. The realization of the fact that I drifted too far into the night prevented me from completing a self-imposed task I thought of embarking on.

I really would like to know the source of that cosmic video that I connected so much to. A video that triggered a long thought process and a couple of weird trance-like rides.

Instinctively, I knew Mary was not the originator of the video. She just posted it—an assertion she eventually confirmed when I contacted her.

At last, I got back home that fateful Monday. It took me a total of thirty-six minutes. I had stopped over at Schnucks to shop for some groceries. That added more minutes to the duration of my trip home. Once home, I changed, went to the gym, came back home, took a shower and swung straight into action—the research on the cosmic video.

The first couple of days after work, I was engrossed in an extensive research on the video and the piece I had transcribed that fateful Sunday night.

At the end of the research, I found out that the transcribed piece was originally written by Carl Edward Sagan. Sagan was an American cosmologist, astrophysicist and astronomer who was renowned for his articulate science communication. Specifically, science communication in astronomy.

Young Carl had shown traits of inquisitiveness about nature from a very tender age. Soon after his mother got him a library card at the age of five, he began to visit the library by himself searching solely for books on stars, the sun and extraterrestrial intelligence.

He excelled at his studies, becoming a straight-A student. Eventually, he was made the president of the school's chemistry club. This position rekindled his interest in science in a tremendous way. He set up his own laboratory at home, where he basically taught himself about molecules and how molecules are formed.

His teachers were astonished by his brilliance and advised his parents to withdraw him and register him at a school for gifted kids. Unfortunately, his parents couldn't afford it. However, without attending a school for the gifted kids, Sagan won several awards while in high school.

He attended the University of Chicago. After his BA degree in 1954, he went on to earn an MS degree in Physics in 1956 as well as a PhD in the Physical Studies of Planets in 1960.

My research further revealed that the script for the voice-over was an excerpt from Carl Sagan's book titled, *Pale Blue Dot*, published in 1994. The images in the video may have been part of the original video that inspired Sagan to write the inspiring piece.

The original image was taken, as requested by Sagan, by Voyager 1 on February 14, 1990 when the spacecraft explored the solar system. Voyager 1 was said to have been around 6.4 billion kilometers (approximately 4 billion miles) away at about 32 degrees above the ecliptic plane when the portrait of Earth was captured. Expectedly, the Earth appeared very tiny right in the middle of scattered light rays, as the picture was taken so close to the sun.

There is no doubt that Sagan lived a fulfilling life as an astronomer and cosmologist. The focus here is not on his laudable achievements in natural science. The focus is rather on the masterpiece he wrote having been inspired by the tiny image of the Earth we all live in.

He wondered why we all hate one another and live our lives placing emphasis on our own strength, our own knowledge, our own ability and our own race.

Ironically, the earth, for now, happens to be the only world where life exists, and Sagan wondered why messages of hatred are taking over messages of love and unity considering the insignificance of the size of the entire Earth when viewed from a distance. It's a small world, as is often said, and as such, there shouldn't be enough space for hate that threatens people's peaceful coexistence. Race isn't a crime—but racism is.

CHAPTER 11:
GLOBAL IDENTITY

A kind gesture can reach a wound that only compassion can heal.

– Steve Maraboli

Over the years, most people erroneously believe that racism only exists in a multi-racial society. Therefore, they tend to hold a wrong perception that a country like the United States of America, for instance, naturally breeds and nurtures the scourge of racism. As a result of this erroneous belief, a majority of the people are of the opinion that racism is an American issue, or an issue peculiar to multi-racial societies, as the case may be.

As a matter of fact, racism is not an American issue or an issue of a specific nation. Racism is a people issue. Racism is universal. Race notwithstanding, people always have that propensity of being erratic. Naturally, they seem to have no challenge shifting focus from an individual's character to being judgmental based on the individual's race or ethnic affiliation.

I've lived in the United States of America close to two decades now and I refuse to see racism as an American issue but as a global issue peculiar to people across the board. I'm a first-generation immigrant originally from Nigeria—a nation super great in human, material and natural resources.

The country shares borders with the Republic of Benin in the west, Cameroon and Chad in the east and Niger in the north. The nation has a long stretch of coastline in the south which lies on the Gulf of Guinea and happens to be the farthest northeastern part of the tropical Atlantic Ocean.

Nigeria is, arguably, the most culturally diverse nation in the entire universe. The country has close to 400 ethnic groups with over 520 languages. For a nation that is as culturally diverse as Nigeria, one would think race would be a unifying factor that would lubricate a strong bond across the length and breadth of ethnicity.

Surprisingly, racism is one of the most worrisome societal menaces that threatens love and unity in that country as well. One strange and bizarre thing about racism is that when it travels from a multi-racial society like the United States of America to a mono-racial society like Nigeria, it blends with the system, embarks on research, and finds out the cultural diversity of the people. Then it changes name from racism to tribalism and operates the same way it operates in a multi-racial society.

Racism has mastered the most effective way of propagating its hate message—a message that has torn the human race apart. A message that has perverted the course of justice across the globe. A message that has permanently placed humans at loggerheads. A message that has dastardly enshrined prejudice, favoritism, cruelty, hatred, murder, bigotry, genocide, xenophobia, apartheid and unnecessary wars among people who are brothers and sisters by extension.

Unfortunately, the human race never realized it. Only a handful is cognizant of the extent of damage perpetuated by racism. Racism has successfully utilized the race factor as a weapon of discrimination in a multi-racial society, and has also cleverly utilized tribalism and ethnic bias as weapons of discrimination in a mono-racial society with multiple tribes and ethnic groups.

In a country where all citizens are of the same race, racism in form of tribalism is the bane of all and sundry. The political elites understand the game. There are no defined rules. The rules are very flexible. Extremely flexible in most cases. The frequency at which the rules change often competes with the number of times the eyes blink. It depends solely on whoever is in power.

For instance, a president mostly appoints members of his tribe to fill political offices, while appointed heads of government parastatals, for the most part, employ folks of the same ethnic descent—"fellow kinsmen," as they are fondly referred to. Regrettably, these lopsided appointments and employments are no doubt at the expense of merit and competence.

At the end of it all, mediocre folks end up in the driver's seat of the nation's affairs with a brazen intent to propagate selfish and tribe-driven interests. Surprisingly, some people still wonder why nations that fall victim to this heinous practice, triggered by tribalism, ethnic prejudice and nepotism, are perpetually retrogressive.

This retrogression eventually became a source of concern to some progressives who have genuine interest in moving the nation past the line of tribalism. For decades, this group, under different auspices, challenged the status quo. They were hopeful that acting against public office-holders who wittingly or unwittingly exhibit the ignoble act of tribalism would make a significant impact. Some of the luminaries of the legal profession even went a step further, requesting that laws be enacted specifically for this purpose just so erring public office-holders could be prosecuted accordingly. According to them, such a step would serve as a deterrent measure to folks with a propensity of prejudice against tribes outside of their tribes.

In no time, several movements sprang up. Media contents were inundated with series of awareness. Accusing fingers began to point in the directions of political elites who either discriminated against people outside of their tribes or ethnic groups or unduly exhibit tribe-driven favoritism.

Eventually, the aims of the movements were achieved—at least partially. An independent federal executive body christened *The Federal Character Commission* was established by Section 153 (1) of the 1999 Constitution.

Primarily, an act that established the commission stipulates, among other things, that the commission shall be saddled with responsibility to *promote, monitor and enforce compliance with the principles of the proportional sharing of all bureaucratic, economic, media and political posts at all levels of government.*

To ensure that the commission is fully autonomous, the act also stipulates that the commission shall not be subject to the *direction, control or supervision of any other authority or person in the performance of its functions.*

In addition, the functions of the commission include working out equitable formula that will act as a template for the distribution of posts (of all cadres) in the public as well as civil service. The same template is expected to contain equitable formula for the distribution of posts in the armed forces and the police force.

Furthermore, the act provides a response to the luminaries' clarion calls for prosecution as it statutorily empowers the commission to take legal measures including the prosecution of the heads of staff of any government ministry, extra-ministerial department or agency that fails to comply with any of the federal character principles or formula prescribed or adopted by the commission.

The emergence of this commission is a proof of the fact that racism is not specific to a multi-racial society. It lends credence to the fact that racism has indeed crept into social and political lives of the people in the form of tribalism. Evidently, this tribalism has ravaged the peaceful coexistence of the people and has successfully divided them on the line of tribe, ethnicity, culture, custom and language.

Unfortunately, the establishment of the *Federal Character Commission* hasn't made a laudable impact. This is partly because the act establishing it failed to make it all-inclusive, if the statutory functions of the commission are anything to go by. Like other similar commissions in most mono-racial nations, emphasis seems to be on the eradication of nepotism at the expense of tribalism and ethnic bigotry.

Regrettably, the situation gets worse as each day rolls by. People from the south detest people from the north. People from the east won't touch people from the midwest with a long pole. People of the same ethnic group can't get along with one another because there is a slight difference in the language they speak.

As a matter of fact, some folks are hypocrites. They have zero tolerance for people outside of their tribes who are obviously of the same skin color. Yet, this same set of people accuse folks who are intolerant of people of other races as racists. What a terrible double standard.

Annoyingly, some extremists will stratify a village whose inhabitants are of the same ethnic group with the same language. Each stratum is then labeled compound, clan or quarters as the case may be. Invariably, at least for the most part, these extremists end up discriminating against folks outside of their quarters. No other form of discrimination could be more heinous.

It is still not clear that the extent of damage arising from tribalism will be quantified anytime soon. Continually, the situation poses a great deal of threat to happiness, unity, love, peaceful coexistence and living life to its fullest. The list of victims is inexhaustible. Some are traumatized, believing they are probably not good enough; while some lose self-esteem thinking their tribes aren't good enough. Actually, some have been sentenced to a life of unhappiness and confined to a permanent state of dejection.

CHAPTER 12:

THE PREPARATION

We are all different. Don't judge, understand instead.

– Roy T. Bennett

Talking about people sentenced to a life of unhappiness and confined to a permanent state of dejection, such is the story of Titilola and Umar. Titilola is a smart young lady. Her parents, Kunle and Biola Olofin, are both of Yoruba extraction from the ancient city of Idanre town.

Yoruba is an ethnic group of southwestern Nigeria. Idanre town in Ondo State, where they are from, is located at the foot of a popular scenic hill that derived its name (Idanre Hill) from the name of the ancient town. The town has a rich cultural heritage that attracts tourists from across the globe. It's one of the significant tourist destinations in Nigeria.

Ironically, Titi, as Titilola is fondly called by friends and family members, never visited the hill. Not even Idanre, her ancestral hometown. She grew up with her parents in Lagos, the commercial nerve center of Nigeria and the most populous city in the continent of Africa. The city of Lagos is ahead of Cairo, Egypt and Kinshasa,

Democratic Republic of the Congo, which happen to be the second and the third most populous cities, respectively.

Kunle, Titi's father, is a successful ophthalmologist who runs one of the largest private clinics in town. Biola, Titi's mother, on the other hand, is also a successful career woman. She's the Director of Corporate Communications of the biggest commercial bank in the country. The bank in question prides itself as the biggest bank in the country by a combination of total deposits and gross earnings.

As a young girl while growing up, Titi always admired the doggedness of both her parents and has consciously paved a different path for herself. She has a desire and an inordinate ambition to improve on her parents' success metrics.

One of the early life lessons she got from her parents was how consequential education is. She was brought up with a strong mentality that education is everything. To her, education precedes success, and success is determined by an individual's desire and ability to acquire formal education. As she nurses a desire to meet up with and surpass her parents' pedigree, she focuses more and more on ways to acquire quality formal education.

Kunle and Biola are devout Christians, non-conformists and strict disciplinarians in that order. They instilled all of these in Titi's mind. Their dream is to have their beloved daughter mirror everything that they are. More than any other thing, it will be right to say Titi was brought up with strong Christian values. There was an in-house schedule for Bible study. The schedule was designed on purpose by Kunle and Biola to spread across all weekdays and weekends. Titi had to show up at every study with a newly memorized verse from the Bible. With this alone, even today, Titi literally became a mobile repository of numerous Bible verses and passages.

Missing Sunday school at church on Sundays was not only inexcusable, but being a couple of seconds late for Sunday school attracted a list of punishments. For the most part, all of the several expectations prepared her for a unique life journey where strict adherence to parental rules and personal temperament crossed paths. However, she designed her own strategy christened *patifoc*.

Titi came up with this word herself. It represents her two guardrails in life: patience and focus. For Titi, patience would immensely assist her to constantly maintain conformity with all the home rules under her parents, while focus will ensure she paves a path to success for herself.

Those guardrails—patience and focus—eventually paid off. Titi's academic performances all through junior and senior high schools were excellent. Aside from being a straight all-distinctions student, she did not fail to complement that with good behavior. As a matter of fact, Titi did not only graduate from high school as the most brilliant, she also carted away a prize as the best-behaved student.

To her teachers and even the non-academic staff of the school, it is extremely rare to find students who combine exceptional academic brilliance with pleasant behavior, but to Titi's parents, the bar should not have been any lower. Kunle and Biola gave an affirmative nod of extreme satisfaction to each other. They took each other on a memory-lane trip.

They remembered how they had carefully drawn a strategy hung on a framework for their beloved daughter: the in-house routine discipline, reward system for good behavior, identifying and avoiding bad company outside the home, show of respect for people, the principles of timeliness, the importance of prayers and putting God first in all endeavors as well as the need to imbibe Christian values at all times.

So, Kunle and Biola had no doubts in their minds that all of these factors, which form the pivot upon which Titi's upbringing swung, contributed immensely to who Titi has turned out to be. Like any parents, they told her how proud they've always been of her.

After a successful high-school graduation, Titi, with her parents' guidance, began to look in the direction of university education. College life has been a dream for Titi since she became a young adult, particularly as her parents already made her believe that life's success was grounded in formal education. For months, her parents went through the list of likely universities with her. They evaluated ratings and courses of study.

Eventually, Titi settled for Ahmadu Bello University. ABU, as the university is fondly referred to in Nigeria, is a federal government research university located in Zaria, Kaduna State. It was founded on October 4, 1962 as the University of Northern Nigeria before being named after Alhaji Sir Ahmadu Bello, the first and the only premier of the Northern Nigeria region who was assassinated on January 15, 1966.

Titi indicated interest in Electrical and Computer Engineering and eventually sat for the university matriculation examination. Expectedly, the period between successful completion of matriculation examinations and release of results is always filled with anxiety. It was not any different for Titi. She had studied hard for the exams like other students. She had also prayed hard, like the typical church girl that she is.

Days rolled into weeks and the results were finally released. Not only did she make it, she also made the list of the top five. Kunle and Biola couldn't have been more proud of their lovely daughter. They shared the good news with friends and family members. It was an unending influx of congratulatory messages for Titi in the days following the release of the matriculation examinations results. The days also witnessed preparations towards becoming an undergraduate, a familiarization tour of the university as well as literally bidding friends farewell.

For Titi, it was a mixed feeling. Excitement on one side and fear of the unknown on the other. Titi realized she had to leave home for the first time. Now, she would have to make unilateral decisions on her own for the most part and learn how to deal with the consequences of her decisions.

She also became worried about the right strategy to adopt in an attempt to maintain the academic standard she had always lived up to. She knew college education was a lot different from what she had heard and read.

At this point, beyond the excitements, she knew she needed no one to remind her that a whole lot of serious work, determination and sleepless nights of hard studies are some of the bumps on the road to successful graduation from college.

Titi had to resume in the first week of October. So, Kunle and Biola were both busy in the weeks prior to the resumption day. Aside from shopping for items on Titi's school list, they had to decide on a drop-off option that worked for the family. Eventually, they chose driving over flying from Lagos to Zaria. To them, driving would give them an opportunity to have more family time. They'll also save on those extra luggage fees for Titi's school items. Besides, they hadn't taken a family road trip in a long time.

They all agreed to hit the road two days prior to resumption day. The plan was for them to take one day of rest in Zaria and head back to Lagos shortly after Titi's scheduled orientation at school was over. Lagos to Zaria is about 698 kilometers (424 miles). So, they left very early in the morning on the day scheduled for the trip. It turned out to be a pleasant trip.

Titi was particularly excited. Aside from the day they flew to Zaria for a familiarization tour of Ahmadu Bello University, she had never been to any northern part of Nigeria. Now, not only was she going to officially sojourn in the north, she also has to learn how to survive all by herself throughout the duration of her studies in an unfamiliar terrain without her parents for the first time.

The orientation was eventful. Kunle and Biola were now ready to leave. They had to make it back to Lagos before it got too dark. Though they planned to get a hotel and set out as early as they could the next morning in case they were unable to make a same-day trip, they still attempted to leave in a timely manner anyway.

Expectedly, it was an emotional departure for Kunle and Biola. They gave Titi one last kiss after a long farewell conversation. For the most part, the conversation was more about last-minute advice on the need for Titi to conduct herself in a manner that would reflect the values they raised her with. Specifically, Kunle laid emphasis on the need for her to always keep caution within reach and not throw it to the winds.

Eventually, it was time to leave. On Biola's suggestion, they all entered inside the car, where they said short prayers. They had the most emotional group hug afterwards, and with tear-filled eyes, Titi bade them farewell. She stood there motionless as she watched her parents drive off out of sight.

CHAPTER 13:

THE MEETING POINT

Our task must be to free ourselves...by widening our circle of compassion to embrace all living creatures and the whole of nature and its beauty.

– Albert Einstein.

Like honey bees in a beehive, ABU students are always busy. From resumption day to the day of final examination for the semester, there are scheduled academic activities that keep students on their toes for the most part. This is the same with most colleges.

Registration for fresh and returning students was underway when Kunle and Biola left. Titi was now officially by herself. Everywhere she turned, there were students carrying files and clipboards containing instructions on the registration process. While it appeared like some knew what they were doing, there was a clear indication that most folks didn't have a clue on what needed to be done or where to go.

Aside from the fresh students, some of the returning students were still clueless as a couple of procedures had either been updated or outrightly changed. The information was overwhelming. You have to sign here. You have to submit paperwork there. You have to check a certain list here. You have to beat a certain deadline there. I'm assuming online registration has now replaced all of these and life is hopefully a lot easier for the students.

Titi stood still. Obviously confused. "Where do I start from?" she asked herself rhetorically.

Just then, a young man walked up to her. "Is everything okay?" he asked. "You must be a *Jambite,*" he observed as Titi struggled to respond to his question. In Nigeria's collegiate parlance, *Jambite* is a popular nickname for freshmen on campus.

"Yes, I'm a Jambite," Titi finally responded, ignoring the young man's first question.

"You'll be alright," the young man assured Titi. "We've all been there," he added. "Please, pardon my manners," he implored as he stretched forth his right hand for a handshake with Titi. "My name is Umar," he announced in the most solemn manner. "I'm a 200-level Chemical Engineering student," he added. By the way, 200 level translates to second year in college. It is similar to *sophomore* in a college in the United States.

"I'm Titilola," Titi said. "Friends and family members call me Titi," she added stretching forth her right hand to accept Umar's handshake. As their fingers locked around their palms, Titi maintained direct eye contact for the first time since Umar walked up to her. "He's good looking," she thought. Coincidentally, Umar felt the same way about Titi.

"So, what are you in school for?" Umar asked. "Is that supposed to be some kind of secret?" he teased. He then told her he noticed how she skipped that part while introducing herself.

"I was going to get to that before you rudely interrupted," Titi responded in what sounded more like a payback tease. They both laughed hysterically. "I'm an Electrical and Computer Engineering student," Titi enthused. "Obviously, a 100-level student," she added jokingly.

"Great, there is a possibility we'll end up attending some general classes," Umar hinted.

After all the initial exchange of pleasantries, Umar, in his usual manner, cleared his throat in an attempt to change the topic. "If you don't mind, I could be of help showing you round the right places where you need to get your registration completed," he volunteered.

With Umar's help, the registration was less strenuous for Titi. She expressed a profound appreciation to Umar for lending a helping hand. She also advised him to open a private consulting firm on campus with the sole aim of providing registration services for new students and confused returning students. "With your wealth of experience with the student-registration process, you'll make some good money. Don't you think?" Titi joked.

"Stop being sarcastic, it won't earn you extra points in any of your classes," Umar replied.

They both laughed and bade each other goodbye. At this time, it felt like they'd known each other for years.

Classes soon began and every student got busy with lectures, late night studies, research, and group and individual assignments. In the middle of all the crazy schedules, it looked more like Umar and Titi couldn't stop seeing each other. From time to time, they agreed to meet at the library, campus restaurants, and some quiet lawns within the campus. As they got closer in their friendship, they discovered that they had a couple of things in common. Most especially their Christian faith. Titi was surprised to find out that some northerners are Christians. In Nigeria, people in the northern part of the country are predominantly Muslims.

Those meetings gave Titi an opportunity to know more about her new friend. Umar's last name was Rufai. He lost his mother at a very tender age and his father took up the challenge of single parenthood, raising Umar and his siblings all by himself. Aliu Rufai was a high-profile contractor who owned an indigenous construction firm in Kaduna. Kaduna is the capital city of Kaduna State in northwestern Nigeria. All tiers of government were essentially Aliu's clientele. As a result, he always hobnobbed with the political elites, as they were the sources of the juicy contracts that made his construction firm a formidable local firm.

Like Titi's parents, Aliu is a devout Christian. He is a fourth-generation Christian, as his great-grandfather converted to Christianity and the faith had always been passed down ever since. Aliu has also successfully passed it on to Umar.

A typical day in the Rufai family starts with a central alarm system that goes off at exactly 5:15 a.m. This alarm sounds across the entire house. Which usually means you have only fifteen minutes to get out of bed, step out of the bathroom or prepare to drop whatever you're doing and converge in the prayer room.

The family prayer time starts at 5:30 a.m., and there is a large courtyard within the house that is designated for morning and night prayer sessions. None of the household members dare show up late, as Aliu takes punctuality very seriously. The entire household is a huge one with Umar and his seven siblings as well as extended family members who live with them.

Weeks rolled into months, and Umar's and Titi's affection for each other became undeniable. It was a natural affection that was simply unexplainable. Interestingly, and expectedly too, they began a relationship having decided to take their friendship to the next level. Before the semester was over, most students on campus did not only know Titi and Umar, they also referred to them as the most popular couple on campus.

Titi and Umar were simply inseparable. You would literally see Umar wherever you found Titi. The best way they spent time outside of schoolwork was being together. They could hardly stay apart from each other for a couple of hours. Umar never stopped telling Titi how much he loved her and how much she meant to him. Titi, in the same vein, never got tired or bored listening to those two lines, which came across to her in diverse, loving ways.

For Titi, these were her first butterflies-in-the-belly feelings. She never experienced what being in love is all about. For Umar, it was a little bit of familiar terrain. He had been in a relationship with a Hausa girl before now. He met this girl named Zarah at an end-of-the-year party organized by a very close business associate of his father.

His dad seemed to have encouraged the relationship, but unfortunately, the relationship didn't stand the test of time. They didn't have that special connection that ensures and breeds affection. Needless to say, the flame went out shortly after it all began.

However, with Titi, it was a different ballgame. He just couldn't explain the feelings, the passion, the affection and the depth of his love for her. Titi was his world. Most of the time, he sat alone in his dorm room and imagined life with Titi after school. Funny enough, Titi struggled with the same imagination whenever she was alone.

The semester soon ended. They both wrote their end-of-semester examinations after hard study. While students were excited to leave school for the semester break, Umar and Titi were sad because they couldn't figure how to survive without each other for the duration of the semester break. Over and over again, they had to face the same ordeal each time school went on break.

How time flies. The semesters had rolled into sessions. It was time for Umar to bid school farewell as he wrote his final examinations. He couldn't believe he had graduated already. "Where on earth did the time go?" he asked as Titi congratulated him. "It was just like yesterday when my dad dropped me off at college for the first time," he remembered.

As they both reminisced over their first day at school and how both of them met in a dramatic way, they laughed and assured each other of their undying and unconditional love. This time, they stayed a bit longer at school after their examinations, as Umar needed to see his project supervisor. For his final-year project, he chose to take a critical look at the effects of temperature on hydrolysis of cellulose and needed some advice from his supervising professor on how to stay within the project's scope.

Eventually, he got all he needed and it was time to leave school. The most difficult for him was having to leave Titi. This time, they would have to face the reality of being apart from each longer than they had ever imagined, as Umar headed back to Kaduna to prepare for the National Youth Service Corps (NYSC) and Titi traveled back to Lagos to spend the break with her parents and prepare for her last session at school.

For Titi, it was the longest break ever. For the first time since she was in college, she didn't really look forward to the next date of resumption, as she realized Umar was not going to be there. It was specifically difficult to process a certainty as real as spending the next session at school without Umar.

Kunle and Biola noticed something different in their daughter. Most especially Biola. She must have been tipped off by mother's instinct. She had a discussion with Kunle about it almost every evening after work.

"Have you noticed something strange with Titi since she came back from school?" Biola quizzed.

"Yeah! I was actually going to talk to you about it. I've noticed that she's just…I don't know. She seems to…" Kunle responded without a definite conclusion.

"It looks more like she's no longer the happy baby she used to be," Biola interrupted. "She stays more in her room, keeps more to herself and it looks more like she's not excited to be home this time," Biola reiterated.

"You know what, sweetheart? I'll let you have a mother-daughter talk with her and let's see if she opens up," Kunle suggested.

That night, Biola waited for the most appropriate time. Unfortunately, the time she planned didn't work out. She had targeted a game show on TV. They all, as a family, had a tradition of watching the game show together. So Biola had planned to talk to Titi immediately after the game show. However, Titi didn't join them for the show. Kunle and Biola could only gaze at each other in disbelief. They knew how much Titi loved to watch the game show with them.

As soon as the show was over, Biola didn't wait to see the end captions scroll down the screen. She headed straight to Titi's room. After a combination of soft and hard knocks on the door with no response, Biola quietly turned the doorknob to the left and pushed the door open, expecting some form of resistance, but the door was not latched from behind.

As she pushed the door open, she noticed Titi on her bed face up literally staring at the ceiling. Biola traced her gaze to the extreme right corner of the ceiling to see if there was any image that caught Titi's attention so much that she didn't even notice her mother had walked into the room. Surprisingly, Biola couldn't find any image. Her worries grew worse as Titi didn't acknowledge or respond to her exchange of pleasantries.

Titi didn't notice she had company in the room until her mother sat on the edge the bed and held her hand. "Good evening, love," Biola greeted as she held Titi's hand.

"Oh! Good evening, mom," Titi finally responded, having been jolted back to life by her mom's physical touch.

"Are you alright?" Biola queried.

"Yes mom. I'm okay," Titi responded, keeping a straight face.

"You don't look okay, my daughter. This is definitely not you."

"Mom, I'm perfectly okay," Titi tried to reassure her mother. "What gave you the impression that something is wrong with me?"

"I'm your mother. Remember? I can tell when something bothers you. You no longer ask questions. You no longer smile. You no longer join me in the kitchen since you came back from school. You didn't even join us for your favorite game show on TV. Yet you need me to believe all is well with you?" she queried.

As a mother, Biola tried all she could to make Titi open up on what the issue with her was, but she just wouldn't budge. At some point, mother's instinct kicked in again for Biola and she asked a question that instantaneously gave her a clue. "Now, tell me Titi. Are you missing him that much?"

At this point, Titi's reaction gave her away. She froze when her mother asked her that question. Her facial expression changed. The straight face she had displayed since her mother came into her room transformed completely into what could be best described as curiosity. She wondered why her mother knew exactly what she had going on. Her eyeballs bulged all of a sudden like they were going to fall off their sockets. She had a weird feeling that the muscles responsible for moving the eyeballs had just suddenly failed.

Biola quickly noticed Titi's facial expression. She needed no one to tell her she guessed right. Before Titi could dismiss her guess, she sprang into action by acting like she had everything under control. She assured Titi that every grown woman she sees around went through a similar emotion at some point. "It's a normal feeling," Biola assured. "Just don't let it hit you too hard and learn how to place that feeling under control," she advised.

That trick worked perfectly well. Titi leaned forward towards her mother. It looked more like she couldn't hide it any more. "How do you place such feeling under control?" she asked passionately.

Biola tactically avoided providing a response to Titi's question. In her mind, she was relieved that it wasn't something too serious going on with her daughter. She never bothered asking to know who the guy was. "We'll talk about how you can make that happen much later. For now, you need to get up and be yourself once again," she suggested as she walked out of Titi's bedroom.

Back in Kaduna, Umar was not having it all easy either. For him, it was an emotional roller-coaster. He was excited that college was over with—at least for his first degree. No more late-night studies. No more hard preparations for examinations. No more anxieties over grades. No more worries about impromptu tests. Unfortunately, there was need for him to now worry some more about Titi. How to cope with missing her? How to make Titi's introduction to his father happen? How to make the long-distance relationship work? Especially now that he was out of school.

These and many more things occupied Umar's thoughts and mind. He hardly paid attention to any other thing that had nothing to do with Titi. Over and over again, he wanted to see her face and hear her voice. He wanted to see that broad smile on her face and talk to her. He just couldn't stop thinking about her. Gradually, he began to develop and display some strange behavioral traits—being absent-minded was one of the most noticeable.

Aliu noticed the new and strange personality traits exhibited by his son. "Your absent-mindedness these days is a huge source of concern for me," Aliu informed Umar on a Sunday afternoon as they got back home from church.

"There's absolutely nothing to worry about, dad," Umar assured him. "I'm all grown now and I have more things to worry about. I'm still working on my final-year project, trying hard to beat the deadlines for submission and defense. I'm also making preparation for NYSC. All of these could take a toll on a young man," he further tried to convince his father.

Umar's reasons seemed to have made sense to Aliu. He nodded in agreement with everything his son said to defend his new behavior. He walked across to Umar and placed his right hand on his left shoulder, with a hope that such a gesture would calm him down a little bit. "You are right, son. All of these could put some weight on you. Just take it easy. One step at a time and all will be alright. Deal?" he concluded as he patiently waited for a response. This was habitual for Aliu. Whenever he advised or gave an order, he always requested to know if it was a deal, just to ascertain his listener was on the same page with him.

"Deal, dad," Umar responded as his father walked away satisfied.

As Aliu made a left into a long walkway that led to his bedroom, Umar stood there motionless. He knew deep down in his heart that he had just lied to his father. Final-year project and preparation for NYSC were the least worries on his mind. Titi and every other thing that had to do with her were the sources of concern for him. First and foremost, he was missing her. Then, he had to constantly engage himself on the need to come up with the right strategies on how to constantly see her during his NYSC year as well as how to introduce her to his father and the rest of the family members.

Eventually, Umar completed his final-year project and proceeded for his NYSC afterwards. He was posted to the old Bendel State (now Edo State). As soon as he obtained his call-up letter from the Students' Affairs Department, he headed straight to one of the telephone booths on campus (there were no cell phones at the time). His heart skipped several beats as he put a call across to Titi's home phone.

They had not talked since school went on break. He tried once from Kaduna and Titi's dad picked up, but Umar was too timid to identify himself and request who he wanted to speak with. He just stood there with the earpiece glued to his left ear. Kunle yelled hello into the mouthpiece a couple of times on the other end, and hung up when he didn't get a response.

This time as the phone rang, he planned to be more of a man. Just then, there was a click sound indicating someone had picked on the other end. All of a sudden, he felt a jerk in his body temperature. His feet began to get cold as the pressure of blood flow to the feet reduced drastically. He instantly forgot his planned and well-rehearsed first statement as he hoped the voice he would hear next would be that of Titi.

He was wrong. It was Titi's mother. "Hello, residence of the Olofins. How may I help you?"

Umar had a habit of clearing his throat before starting a conversation or responding to a question. On this fateful day, his throat seemed to have been congested from a combination of fear and confusion. He knew an attempt to clear his throat might irritate whoever was at the other end. Having lost out on his planned first statement if anyone aside from Titi picked the receiver, he slipped his right hand in his pants pocket, and fumbled a little with the receiver with his left hand in an attempt to display some form of confidence.

"Hello ma'am," he finally spoke almost confidently while displaying a weird gesture with his facial expression as he frantically searched his mind blankly for his next statement.

"I presume I'm speaking with Mrs. Olofin," he murmured.

"Yes, this is she," Biola confirmed. "Who am I speaking with please?" She asked rather inquisitively.

"My name is Umar," he announced.

"U...what?" Biola asked.

"Umar," he repeated.

"Have we met?" She queried.

"Not exactly, ma'am. I'm Titi's friend from ABU," he explained.

"Oh! Okay," Biola responded.

"May I please speak with her, ma'am?" Umar requested, trying to be as unobtrusive as he could be.

"Sure. She's in. Hold on one second, please," Biola said as she yelled Titi's name.

"There is an Usman on the line for you," Biola informed Titi as she literally raced into the living-room area.

As her mother handed her the receiver, she knew it was Umar. Her mom had erroneously assumed she heard the young man introduce himself as Usman. She ignored her mother's mistake, as all that mattered to her was the fact that she was about to hear the voice of someone she had missed so much.

It was somewhat of a lengthy conversation between Umar and Titi. They had so much to catch up with. The call-up letter, the project and the state he was posted to for his service year, Titi's final year schedule as well as other topics salient to them. They expressed how much they missed each other. However, Titi wondered why he hadn't called as agreed earlier. Umar then shared the story of his encounter with her father on phone and they both laughed hysterically about it. Afterwards, Umar reeled out his plans on how to frequently visit her at school during his service year.

Titi couldn't be more satisfied with Umar's plans. Especially, his plans to frequently travel to school to visit her. That meant a lot to her. She felt a lot better after their telephone conversation. Once again, she gradually transformed into the Titi that her parents had known all along.

Her mother particularly felt elated at having her daughter back. She wondered what it was that jolted her back to life? She thought whatever it was sure made a tremendous difference. Strange enough, as attentive as she was, she never suspected the phone call from Umar did the trick.

CHAPTER 14:

NURTURE

Compassion is the basis of morality.

– Arthur Schopenhauer

Weeks went by. Biola had resumed in school for a new semester that kicked off her last session. Every other thing stayed the same—the classes, individual and group assignments, quizzes and tests as well as late-night studies. The only thing different this time was the fact that Umar was no longer part of the school routine. She missed him so much.

Umar went for his service year as expected. Preceding the service year was a mandatory three-week orientation usually held at the orientation camp of the state the corps member was posted to. The orientation camp was quite eventful. Very eventful—the parades, the dramas, the excitement, sanitation, cooking, debates, broadcasts, sports, fire night, endurance trek and much more.

The orientation camp was, no doubt, fun-filled. The only exception was that you had to prepare for the regimented life at the camp. You literally had to wake up at a certain time, come out for parades at a specific time, and have breakfast, lunch and dinner at certain times. For Umar, it was not too difficult an adjustment. After all, he had to wake up at a specific time for early-morning prayers at the prayer room in his father's house.

Three weeks soon rolled by and it was time to prepare for resumption at primary places of assignments. For primary place of assignment, Umar was posted to a high school in the ancient city of Benin City. Benin was the capital city of the old Bendel State (now the capital city of Edo State). The city is about 200 miles east of Lagos and 25 miles north of the Benin River. The indigenous people of Benin are referred to as the Edo People, and they speak the Edo language.

Also known as Benin Kingdom, the city was an integral part of a pre-colonial kingdom which is now known as southern Nigeria. It (the kingdom) was annexed in 1897 by the British Empire and prides itself as one of the oldest in the coastal hinterland of West Africa.

Umar can't wait to travel to Zaria to see Titi at School. He wasted no time reporting at the high school he was posted to. He had a meeting with the school principal alongside two other corps members posted to the school. At the meeting, Umar made a case for himself. He informed the principal of the need for him to take a trip before settling down finally. The principal was very cooperative and promised to arrange for a substitute. It was reconfirmed during the meeting that Umar would take the students in Mathematics and Chemistry.

The school had a hall of residence for corps members, popularly referred to as Corpers' Lodge. It was built more like detachable cabins. A nonacademic associate from the principal's office volunteered to show them round the school and eventually took them to the Corpers' Lodge.

As soon as Umar was ushered into his room, he tidied up and packed items needed for his planned trip in a suitcase. He had earlier asked the nonacademic associate who showed him his room how to get around in the city. He specifically requested to know how to find his way to Kaduna-Zaria Bus Station.

It was the longest night ever for Umar. He stared blankly at the ceiling for most of the night. He was ready as early as four a.m. At five a.m., Umar was already at the bus station. The distance between Benin and Zaria was 437 miles (approximately 712.8 km). He was the first passenger on the bus. Other passengers soon arrived, and the bus eventually moved at the scheduled time of 6:30 a.m.

It was such a long trip for Umar. They stopped at some of the major cities to have restroom breaks, relax or buy some snacks from the parks or roadside hawkers. Each stop took an average of 20 minutes. About 80 percent of the passengers were Kaduna-bound. Eventually, they arrived at Zaria. Umar remained calm as passengers asked questions endlessly from the driver, ranging from requesting directions to their destinations to asking for major landmarks. He assisted as much as he could. He sure knew his way around Zaria pretty well.

Umar remained in the bus until they got to the last bus stop. It was a station not too far from ABU Campus. All he could think of at that moment was Titi. How would she feel seeing him fulfill his frequent visits promise for the first time? He had earlier booked a reservation at the guest house on campus. The front desk associate handed him the keys to his room. As soon as he got into the room, Umar went straight to the bathroom, where he had a quick shower and headed straight to Titi's room.

Titi's roommate informed him that she was not in the room at the time he checked. Umar looked at the time and knew exactly where Titi would be. He thanked Titi's roommate and left with a promise to check on her much later. As soon as the door closed behind him, he went straight to one of the quiet study centers that happened to be one of their favorite places to hang out.

The study center used to be a detached building that was a secretariat of the Students' Union Government (SUG). As he walked past the last block of cafeteria before the study center, he remembered how he held Titi's hands every time they walked to the study center and every time they walked back. He also remembered the last conversation they had when they stopped right at the spot he had just walked past.

On that spot, Titi had stopped to ask him a question. "Now that you're getting ready to leave ABU, I hope out of sight is never going to be out of mind for you?" Titi asked, looking straight into his eyes.

"You already know the answer," Umar quickly responded. "Out of sight is never going to happen in the first place, let alone allowing out of mind to creep in," Umar added at the time.

As he approached the east entrance of the study center, he looked through one of the side windows and saw Titi on the far end of the room to the right. It was their favorite corner. She positioned a chair in front of her where she vertically placed her legs covered with a light blanket to keep the bugs away. She didn't notice as Umar approached. She was engrossed in whatever it was she was reading.

Eventually, Umar was right behind her. He thought of several things he could possibly do—a prank being one of them. However, he quickly dismissed the idea of a prank, as that could possibly distract other students who were studying. He stood there for another minute, or maybe two, and then placed his left hand gently on her right shoulder. "Who could this possibly be?" she thought as she turned around.

As soon as she sighted Umar, the scream was out of this world. She screamed at the top her voice. The chair on which she placed her legs fell over as she attempted to get up on her feet, flinging the blanket on the window frame beside her. Eventually, she got up and literally threw herself at him. He caught her almost midway in the air and gently placed her feet on the ground as they had a long hug. It was such a long hug with an uncontrollable display of excitement and affection.

As they disengaged from each other, Titi realized they were not alone. At this time, all the students in the room already fixed their gaze on them. They had obviously disturbed everyone. Titi felt bad. "I'm so sorry, please," Titi apologized to everyone as she picked up her books and looked around for the blanket. "Over by the window," Umar said, pointing in the direction where the blanket landed when she flung it.

Umar helped her with the books as he always did whenever they were done reading. They left the room to avoid causing more distractions. As soon as they moved out of the study room, Titi was all over him, asking question after question. "How was your trip? How was the orientation camp? How is Benin? Do you like the city? How is your dad? How are your siblings?

Umar laughed a little uncontrollably. "Could you please highlight the first question you need me to answer and arrange others in order of preference?" Umar asked jokingly. They both laughed about this as Titi realized she had asked too many questions. "I'll sure tell you everything you need to know," Umar promised as they walked towards Titi's hostel.

It was such a great reunion for both of them as they talked extensively about events that had unfolded since the last time they spoke on phone. They caught up on so many things. They covered more topics than ever before. He reopened his plans to take Titi home and introduce her to his family. Titi was all in on the plans. Umar ended up spending one week with Titi before leaving for Kaduna to see his father and siblings. He spent three days at home in Kaduna, and eventually left for Benin.

Umar was fascinated by a lot of things in the ancient city of Benin. Specifically, he was impressed by the people's rich culture. It was a huge culture shock for a young man who had to live outside of northern Nigeria for the first time in his life; not only did he try to blend as quickly as possible, but he also made frantic efforts at learning some aspects of the culture.

All year, Umar taught Mathematics and Chemistry. The students liked him, not only because of his depth of knowledge but because he also had special ways of imparting that knowledge. All through the duration of his sojourn in Benin, Umar never broke his promise to Titi. He visited her at school as frequently as he could, especially whenever his students went on break. All his students knew he had a soulmate as he had her pictures on his table and on his wall corner at the teachers' common room. They always noticed a rare enthusiasm that radiated all around Umar each time he had an opportunity to talk about Titi. They knew he was genuinely in love with her.

He once shared with his students how he planned to propose to Titi after his service year. All the students looked up to him. They all dreamed of completing their college education someday and acting exactly like Umar. He had become a role model of a sort to them. They liked everything about him. From his deep knowledge of the subjects he taught them to his sincerity, commitment and faithfulness to Titi.

How time flies! The service year was over. One full year was gone. The passing-out ceremony for the corps members was very colorful. In attendance were top government functionaries. On one of Umar's numerous visits to Titi, they had a discussion about Titi's possibility of attending the passing-out ceremony. Unfortunately, Titi's final examinations at school coincided with the date scheduled for the passing-out ceremony. So there was absolutely nothing they could do about it.

After the passing-out ceremony, Umar left Benin for Zaria, hoping to be there with Titi as she wrote her final papers. The high school offered him full-time employment, but he declined. He thought accepting the offer might ruin his chances of being with Titi. He thought the only reason he would accept the offer would be if Titi was posted to Bendel State for her service year. With slim chances of that happening, he was not ready to take the job-offer bait. Besides, he wanted a more challenging opportunity as a Chemical Engineer.

He got to Zaria just in time and connected with Titi, who just finished her last papers a day earlier. He took her outside of the campus for a romantic dinner in town. *Zippon* was more than a restaurant. It was classy joint on its own based on menu style, methods of meal preparation and service as well as pricing. It attracted the crème de la crème in the Zaria area.

Umar planned in advance for this day. He wanted to be a man. He wanted to impress Titi. He made sure he never asked his father for money for this purpose. He had saved for that day during his service year. He held Titi's hand as they stepped into the customers' lounge and settled on a couch by a large globe and a huge vase.

The vase was a wonder to behold. It was metallic with a decent gold-plait design. It held a beautiful tulip that could take one's breath away. For real. It was a beautiful tulip that appeared more to have been specially grown, as it had protruding inside layers that were tucked inside the outside layers. On the front side of the vase was a drawing more like checkers with a mosaic touch that gave visitors to the restaurant some optical illusions.

Just as they wondered if the tulip was real or artificial, a hostess appeared, introduced herself and ushered them into a dining parlor for two. The parlor was simply gorgeous. It was about 100 square feet. It had a floating table partially attached to the wall. The floating table was designed with flexibility of sitting in mind. Guests could choose to face each other from across the table or sit side-by-side around the table. It had a dark brown marble laminate top that looked more ceramic.

On the extreme left corner were well-arranged *Kalanchoe gastonis-bonnieri* flowers from the *Crassulaceae* family. They covered the crevices of the lower part of the wall as they beautifully adorned the middle of the wall. There was a painting of the eighteenth-century city of Zaria hung on the left side of the wall as well as a large portrait of Queen Amina on the opposite wall.

Titi walked across the sparkling clean dining parlor to take a closer look at the portrait. She remembered everything about Queen Amina from History class back in high school as she admired the portrait. In pre-colonial Nigeria, Queen Amina of Zaria was a formidable force to reckon with. In a male-dominated society, she was the first woman to become the *Sarauniya* (queen). Queen Amina was solely responsible for the unprecedented expansion of the territory of the Hausa people of North Africa to its largest borders ever. She was said to have been born in 1533 in Zaria.

She had lived about 200 years before the establishment of the popular Sokoto Caliphate, an Islamic state founded in 1804 by Uthman dan Fodio (sometimes spelled Usman dan Fodio), who eventually became the first Sultan of Sokoto. Queen Amina assumed the reign over her people (the kingdom), having acquired and demonstrated tremendous military skills that won her military accolades as well as great wealth.

As Titi ruminated over the bravery, influence and success story of Queen Amina, the hostess came in. She unknowingly halted Titi's thought process. With a bent arm, she walked towards the floating table. Titi also walked towards the table behind her in quick succession hoping she wouldn't miss any announcement.

"I do hope everything is okay," the hostess asked professionally as she stretched her bent left arm revealing two menus. She grabbed the menus with her right hand, handed one over to Umar and placed the other conspicuously on the edge of the table.

"Everything is okay," Titi answered with some sort of courtesy to appreciate the hostess' care for her guests. "That portrait right there sure brings back some memories from my high-school History classes," Titi explained, pointing in the direction of Queen Amina's portrait.

"Oh that! I get that a lot from our patrons. She was such a brave lady," the hostess responded, lending a credence to Titi's admiration of the queen.

As Titi made attempts to sit, Umar got up and pulled the seat out for her. As she thanked Umar for that gesture, the hostess picked up the menu she had earlier placed on the edge of the table and respectfully handed it over to Titi. Then she took their orders for drinks and left the dining area as Umar and Titi flipped through the pages of the menus.

The menu paraded an array of local, continental and oriental cuisines. It was a little overwhelming for Titi. She had so many options and found it extremely difficult to make up her mind. She was obviously not alone, as Umar was also indecisive. They sought each other's opinion.

For Titi, it was a break from the monotonous rice with beans and fried plantains that most female students ordered at campus cafeterias. So, if she had to order anything, it had to be a combination of something not available on campus and something she couldn't easily prepare at home, or some kind of meal with a hard-to-find recipe.

For Umar, on the other hand, the mission at *Zippon* was more than the food experience. He had a different plan, so he cared less about his choice. As they talked about possible meal choices, the hostess came in with their drinks. It was cranberry with no ice for Titi and fruit punch with ice for Umar.

"Can I take your meal orders now?" the hostess asked, with an assumption that they had made up their minds.

"Ladies first," Umar said solemnly.

"I'll go with the baked mushrooms and spinach," Titi announced.

"Good choice. You will enjoy it," the hostess said, smiling, as she turned to Umar to take his order.

"Can I have the chicken and cheese salad, please?" Umar requested.

"Sure," the hostess responded. "Please, feel free to let me know if you need anything before your meals," she added as she walked away.

Just then, Umar got up and informed Titi he needed to use the restroom. He came back several minutes later. Titi felt the restroom break was a little long, but decided not to make him uncomfortable by asking question about it. She then brought up a new topic as soon as Umar got back.

She told him how much of a "schoolgirl" she had been all through the duration of her studies at ABU. She was right about that assertion. She had actually been a schoolgirl all along. She hardly went to town and still couldn't find her way around town. She didn't even know a place as beautiful as *Zippon* existed. Indeed, it was her first time in that part of town in the entire four years she had been in Zaria.

"You should have gone out some more," Umar opined. "Anyway, the most important thing right now is that you're now officially a college graduate," he said, trying hard to change the topic. Umar seemed to have succeeded as their discussion now focused on all the hard work and sacrifices it took for their college education journey to be completed.

Just a few minutes into their discussion, the hostess approached the floating table with their ordered meals. On her left hand was a stainless-steel tray and on her right hand was a long feather-weight mobile stool. As she announced the arrival of their meals, she placed the stool on the floor from across the table and set the tray right on the stool. Titi noticed that the dishes were all covered with ceramic lids that looked more like oversize bowls. She thought whatever that was must have been part of *Zippon's* unique services.

The hostess ignored the surprise on Titi's face and gently lifted the dishes from the tray and placed them on the table, sliding Umar's onto his side of the table as well as Titi's. "Enjoy your meal," she said as she headed towards the kitchen area. As soon as the hostess was out of sight, Umar got up, placed Titi's dish right in front of her, and went back to his side of the table afterwards.

He opened the ceramic lid on his food as he closely kept an eye on Titi. A sweet aroma from his chicken and cheese salad accompanied the fresh air that blew straight into Titi's nostrils. As her olfactory nerves picked up the sweet smell, her eyes stayed focused on the meal Umar had just opened. It was an interestingly sparkling salad with tender chicken breasts, well mixed and tossed in salt, pepper and mayonnaise—a very generous dose of it.

Titi almost drooled gazing at Umar's meal. She tried hard not to. It would have, no doubts, been an embarrassment. Unknown to her, Umar had cleverly taken intermittent looks at her. He had been watching out for the moment Titi would flip the lid on her food open.

Finally, Titi was done gazing covetously at Umar's food. She turned over to the dish in front of her—her supposed ordered food. She held the knob-like handle in the middle of the lid and then flipped it open. Surprisingly, there was absolutely no food in the covered dish. No mushroom and spinach. No food. No aroma.

She was confused. She checked the inside of the lid in a manner reminiscent of a victim of a mind trick frantically trying to solve the mystery behind what looked more like a prank. If she had expected to find some strands of spinach stuck to the roof of the lid she had just looked at, she must have been disappointed some more. With all the drama that just unfolded, she felt so stupid realizing there was no steam from a hot meal on the inside of the lid.

Umar watched the thirty-two second drama, pretending he was busy munching on his meal. At some point, Titi's eye caught something tiny in the middle of her empty dish. It was a box holding an engagement ring. Surprised, she turned to look at Umar. By this time Umar was already on his feet. He stretched over and grabbed the box. Then, he went down on bended knees, popped the box open, and ripped an engagement ring off the tiny dock designed to hold the ring inside the box.

Umar proudly and confidently brandished the ring held by his thumb and index finger on the right hand. It was a 14-carat rose gold rounded French-cut diamond ring. He had saved for what he described as an all-important purchase during his service year. Before Titi could recover from the shock, Umar began to tell her how much she meant to him. How he had always felt about her since they met. How he would relinquish anything in an attempt to spend the rest of his life with her, and how he always felt incomplete whenever they were several miles away from each other.

Everything he said to Titi while on his knee was a powerful rendition of his love for her. Afterwards, he requested to know if she would marry him. Their eyes met after Umar had asked the question. There was a long silence—a deafening silence as they gazed at each other. For Titi, it was a combination of excitement from being so loved by someone she loved so much as well as processing Umar's dramatic and romantic proposal.

Eventually, Titi responded with a resounding yes accompanied by an affirmative nod. Umar couldn't conceal his excitement. He got up, hugged Titi and whispered some sweet coherent assurances of love into her ears. At this time, the hostess had shown up, not only with Titi's real meal, but with some of the *Zippon* employees on duty. They all clapped, congratulated and wished Titi and Umar well. Umar appreciated their gesture and thanked them profusely.

As soon as the restaurant employees left, he told Titi how he had planned with the hostess and the manager of *Zippon* Restaurant to make the proposal happen. All that plan with the hostess and the manager happened when he told Titi a few minutes earlier that he needed to use the restroom. "I should have suspected you when your restroom break took an unusually long time," Titi said. She went on to tell him how she didn't want to make him uncomfortable by asking him questions about staying too long in the restroom.

All along Umar knew in his mind that at some point he would have to propose to Titi based on how strongly he felt about her. He had thought it would happen after he introduced Titi to his father and also met Titi's parents. Unfortunately, the long-distance issue they had sure broke the planned sequence. They talked about this and both agreed that now that they were engaged, it made more sense to focus more seriously about meeting each other's parents as well as expediting action towards making that happen.

"You must be hungry by now," Umar said as he got up to help Titi open her real meal. It was her originally ordered food this time. Underneath the lid was a creamy white sauce, poured over mushrooms and spinach sautéed together in butter, topped with slices of tomato with some shredded broiled chicken and served with a toasted baguette. It looked more like a brunch. She loved the taste of the food, but the way she ate indicated she had lost her appetite for the meal as a result of the overwhelming excitement. She had every reason to be excited: she was a brand-new college graduate and a newly engaged young lady.

CHAPTER 15:

DEAD END

If we have no peace, it is because we have forgotten that we belong to each other.

– Mother Teresa

Umar seemed to have come of age now. He had several roles to play. In his mind, he felt very strongly that in addition to playing the role of a reliable son to his father and a dependable brother to his siblings, now he had to add the roles of being a responsible fiancé to Titi as well as a prospective trustworthy son-in-law to his fiancée's parents. To make this happen, he knew he needed to add the role of an innovative, effective and efficient employee at a very promising firm as soon as possible.

Aside from his desire to be with Titi, Umar had an inordinate ambition of being an entrepreneur. However, it was crystal clear to him that he had to start from being an employee first if garnering experience was anything to go by. His father had promised to introduce him to some of his politician friends. He believed his son could always get his dream job through his connections.

Deep inside him, he wanted Umar to be a politician, and he would try all he could to personally hand him over to a trusted politician friend for all the necessary grooming. However, Umar had a different plan. He never wanted to be a politician and wouldn't want to leverage his father's connections for a job. He would rather make it happen all by his own efforts.

Before the end of his service year, he designed a resume that he had been sending out to reputable firms. His doggedness soon paid off, as he got a job offer as an Associate Engineer in a firm in the city of Abuja. It was in the early years of the development of the city. Abuja would eventually become the capital city of Nigeria on December 12, 1991 during the administration of Ibrahim Badamasi Babangida, popularly known as IBB, the then Military President of Nigeria.

At the time, Abuja was a haven of fresh opportunities. It was a city that was centrally located, planned and built in the 1980s and had become the political headquarters of the nation, having been named the beneficiary city of the transfer of the seat of power from Lagos. Before December 12, 1991, Lagos was both the economic and political capital city from 1914.

The new status of the city of Abuja as the capital city of Nigeria witnessed massive relocations of people and all the federal government establishments to the city as well as an unprecedented influx of private firms.

Umar accepted the job offer. To him, it was a first step towards being a full-blown man and a giant step towards being with Titi for the rest of his life. Another good thing for him was that Abuja was not far from Kaduna—198.52 km (123 miles).

Titi was posted to Rivers State for her service year. Just like Umar, Titi had a great deal of fun at the orientation camp. For her, it was such a wonderful experience to serve one's country and learn about other people's culture and way of life. After the mandatory three weeks at the orientation camp, Titi was posted to the city of Port Harcourt for her primary place of assignment.

Port Harcourt is the Capital City of Rivers State. It was founded around 1912 and named after Lewis Harcourt, a British politician of the Liberal Party who happened to be the Secretary of State for the colonies from 1910 to 1915.

The city lies on the coastal line of Bonny River, which happens to be an eastern distributary of River Niger. It is about 66 kilometers (41 miles) upstream from the Gulf of Guinea. The city of Port Harcourt is also a port town and prides itself as the garden city with a large number of multinational firms mainly in the petroleum industry as well as other industrial concerns.

All through the duration of Titi's service year, Umar flew frequently back and forth from Abuja to Port Harcourt to visit her. Titi had also visited Umar in Abuja a couple of times, and on each occasion she had flown to Lagos to spend time with her parents before heading back to Port Harcourt.

By this time, Titi's parents were both aware that she was in a relationship with some guy who lived in Abuja. In the same vein, Umar's father knew that Umar was seriously committed to a smart young lady he met in college.

As soon as service year was over for Titi, she and Umar began to execute their plans. The first step was to have Umar come to Lagos to meet Titi's parents, and then have Titi come over to Kaduna to meet Umar's father and siblings, and then plans for their wedding would kick off afterwards. They had both agreed on the type of wedding they wanted and they had also picked a tentative date.

The plan was for Umar to meet Titi's parents the second week of the month Titi got back home after her service year. They agreed on a Sunday afternoon. This was Titi's idea. She knew her father was always in a very good mood on Sundays. Kunle is always a very happy man, but there was something about Sundays that seemed to amuse him all the time. So Titi couldn't think of a better day for her father to meet her fiancé.

As Titi looked forward to the second week of the month she came back home, she hoped she could fast-forward the days ahead. The Saturday preceding that fateful Sunday was uniquely different for her. It was a Saturday unlike any other. She woke up with a mental image of everything that would happen the next day.

She had imagined Umar walk into the house and her parents welcoming him like their own son. She imagined a well-cultured exchange of warm pleasantries. She imagined Umar's intelligent responses to all her parents' questions. She just imagined and imagined as she felt those butterflies in the belly almost all day.

Umar felt the same way. He flew in from Abuja and checked into a hotel. He had booked a hotel not too far away from Titi's parents' home. He had heard a lot about the crazy and unpredictable Lagos traffic and wouldn't want to risk showing up late. To him, first impressions usually last longer.

As soon as he checked in, he placed his suitcase beside the left night stand, took off his shoes and flung them right by the media chest from across the bed. He quickly looked around the room and then went straight to the bathroom, where he had a warm shower.

For him, that night was the longest night ever. He had no plan to order dinner, as he didn't feel like eating anything. He had no appetite for food at all since he had an early breakfast. He knew exactly what was responsible for his loss of appetite. It was the night before he would meet his prospective parents-in-law for the first time. His mind shuttled between fears and anxiety. He tossed from one edge of the bed to the other as he rehearsed his in-between conversation speeches and responses to likely questions.

It was already early in the morning before he knew it. He barely had four hours of sleep. From previous discussions with Titi, he knew exactly when her parents would leave home for church and when they would make it back home. Since the meeting was scheduled for after church service, he went through the list of the cab service companies the front desk attendant at the hotel handed him at the time he checked in.

He flipped through the list and picked one of the companies randomly. He did not only make a reservation for a ride, he called the company intermittently to ensure a timely arrival of his ride. It's one of the numerous qualities Titi loved about him—punctuality.

Umar dressed up ahead of time. He detested lateness. He took his time to look good and sharp in typical traditional Hausa attire. He had on a blue *Baban Riga* paired with immaculate white *Jalabia* and *Juanni* robes that had a very simple but beautiful embroidery from the collar region down to the upper front button area. As he stood in front of the bathroom mirror adjusting his hat, the telephone in his room rang. As he picked the receiver, the front desk attendant announced the arrival of his ride. "I'll be there in a minute," Umar said. He then replaced the receiver after expressing his appreciation to the front desk attendant.

He took one last gaze in the mirror, slid his wallet into the right side pocket of his pants and adjusted his *Baban Riga* as he pushed the door open. He fumbled through his chest pocket to be sure he had the keys to the hotel room, and once he confirmed that, he headed towards the elevators through the long walkway. He was right on time by the elevators as one of the doors to the elevator opened for a guest. Umar stepped right in and pressed the lobby button as the guest stepped out.

When the doors opened on the ground floor, a professionally dressed chauffeur was already waiting for him. He had on black pants, white shirt, black tie, black coat and a matching cadet-like hat. As soon as Umar appeared, he saved him the stress of looking around for the right guy. He jammed his hands right behind himself in a crisscross manner as he approached Umar.

"Na you be Mr. Rufai?" he asked Umar.

"Yes, I'm Mr. Rufai, but you can call me Umar," Umar replied.

"My name na Oliver," the chauffeur introduced himself. He quickly added that he was the assigned driver to Umar that afternoon. Oliver spoke Pidgin English but sometimes tried to pick up English and always ended up code-switching most of the time.

"Thanks for being so timely, Oliver," Umar commended him as he requested to know where he parked the car.

"Na the main entrance," Oliver responded. He was not new to the hotel. He had picked up and dropped off passengers at the hotel several times, so he was familiar with the designated pick-up area by the main entrance of the hotel.

"You no get luggage?" Oliver wondered.

"I do have luggage, but I'm not checking out at this time," Umar explained, adding that he just wanted to have a quick meeting somewhere. He felt telling Oliver he wanted to meet with his fiancée's parents was not necessary. He considered it as too much information for a guy he just met.

"Where we dey go?" Oliver asked.

"Here." Umar handed him the address. Oliver knew exactly where the area was. They only needed to locate the house number. It was a smooth ride. Oliver and Umar had a good conversation. They discussed the pros and the cons of military government vis-à-vis civilian government. They didn't have time to switch topics as the distance from the hotel to Titi's parents' house was not too far.

They eventually took an exit that led to Titi's neighborhood and Umar's heart began to skip beats as they made a left turn into Titi's street. Oliver had no issue locating the house number. It was a beautiful gated building at the end of the street. Titi's room was upstairs at the west end of the building. Her windows overlooked the gate. She was always the first person to see her parents' guests. She would look through her window to catch a glimpse of whoever was visiting anytime the indoor intercom connected to the gate beeped.

To her, on this fateful day, the family was going to host the most important guest. For the most part, she was in her bedroom with a fixed gaze on the gate through the window. That fixed gaze had been intermittent since they all came back from church. Every now and then, she would have that unexplainable butterfly-in-the-belly feeling.

For the umpteenth time, Titi looked through the window once again. Just as she was about to turn around for the next gaze at the gate, which would have typically been in another 30 seconds going by the frequency at which she checked the gate, she noticed a car slowly pull up at the gate. As the passenger side front door opened, Titi needed no one to tell her that the occupant of the passenger seat was Umar.

As soon as she saw Umar, she let go of the window blind and ran out of her bedroom. She screamed as she sprinted through the walkway that led to the living room and headed straight for the stairs. It was the shortest amount of time she covered the distance between her bedroom and the stairway. Umar walked briskly towards the neatly painted pillar by the gate. He was about to press the black button-like knob on the intercom device on the gate to announce his arrival when Titi flung the gate open, ran towards him and jumped straight into his waiting stretched-out arms.

After a quick exchange of pleasantries, Titi requested to know if the direction to her parents' house was straightforward enough. Umar nodded in the affirmative as she held his hand and ushered him through the gate to the main building.

"How about the gentleman?" Titi asked, referring to the chauffeur.

"Oh, Oliver will have to wait until I finish with my parents-in-law to be," Umar responded, adding that the wait was part of the contract.

"Great," Titi enthused as she reached for the door leading to the main living room.

As soon as they entered the living room, she took Umar to the closest couch to the coffee table and asked him to feel comfortable. Then she went inside to get her parents. She had cleverly planned the sitting arrangement just so she could get a vantage point to clearly view her parents' discussion session with Umar.

She re-emerged in the living room after a couple of minutes— this time, with her parents. Biola and Kunle walked in behind their daughter hand-in-hand in a manner that implied a "this is what is expected of both of you after several years of marriage" kind of message to Umar and Titi. Though it was expected to be some kind of subtle message, Umar got it anyway. He seemed to be pleased with what he saw as he rose to his feet from the couch as a sign of respect for his parents-in-law to be.

A blind man could tell that everyone was excited even with no word said yet. Apparently, Titi was the most excited. She broke the silence. "Mom, dad, meet my fiancé, Umar."

"Umar who?" Biola asked, as she thought within herself that the name did not sound like a Yoruba name or a Christian name. By now, she had quickly assessed Umar's traditional attire and mentally placed the name Umar beside the attire and began to melt internally. "I hope it's not what I'm thinking," she said in Yoruba language to Kunle.

"Umar Rufai," Titi responded to her mother's question, hoping that her response would satisfy her mother's inquisitiveness.

She was wrong. "Ru…what?" Biola fired back. She immediately turned to Umar and requested to know where he was from.

"Kaduna," Umar answered.

"You are Hausa—right?" Biola asked in quick succession.

"Yes, ma'am," Umar responded courteously.

Within a split second, Biola's mood had gone through bouts of transition. From the moment she walked into the living room hand-in-hand with her husband, to the moment she heard Umar say "Kaduna" and admit he was Hausa, she had gone from excitement to curiosity and now to disdain. She obviously lost control of her emotions.

She turned to Titi and literally yelled "We need to talk" at the top of her voice as she walked out of the living room.

Kunle was right behind her as they both headed to their bedroom with Titi watching in total disbelief. She stood there with her feet glued to the laminate floor of the living room. She had no explanation for the drama she just saw. It was the loud sound from her parents' bedroom door that jolted her back to life. Apparently, Biola had closed the door behind her angrily.

At this time, Titi turned to Umar, who was completely speechless and embarrassed, and with tear-filled eyes, she requested that he gives her a couple of minutes to see her parents inside.

As soon as Titi entered her parents' bedroom, Biola wasted no time continuing from where she stopped before leaving the living room out of anger. She ranted and then ranted all over again. She expressed how disappointed she was with Titi's decision, laying emphasis on how much she detested the Hausa people. Eventually, she ended up blaming herself, in part, for not requesting to know Umar's tribal identity at the time she got wind of their relationship.

Titi was overwhelmed with mixed feelings. She never saw this other side of her mother. She cried profusely and turned to her father for support. If she was disappointed and surprised by her mother's actions, she was more than shocked when she discovered that her father sided with her mother.

"Your mom is right, Titi," Kunle announced. "What came over you? We did not send you to the university to bring home a Hausa boy."

Those words pierced Titi's heart and left a large hole in it. She dropped on the floor and cried some more. Kunle and Biola paid no attention to her feelings. They continued to batter and bruise her emotions by describing the amount they were disappointed in her in superlatives. She cried and sobbed in between her parents' long rendition of their unacceptance speech—a well-detailed speech about Umar's total unacceptability.

Titi had heard enough. She got up, wiped her face and cleared her throat as she struggled to find her words. For the first time in her entire life, she stood up to her parents.

"This is not how you raised me," Titi began. "You raised me to love everyone and never to discriminate. You raised me to stand for what I want. I imbibed Christian values with emphasis on loving God and others because you raised me that way. You never told me tribe is an exception to loving others. You never..." she started to make her next point when her mother cut in.

"Keep quiet," she cautioned her daughter. "What do you know about love? What exactly do you know about love?"

"Everything, mom. Everything," Titi answered confidently. "I know enough about love to realize that it makes the world go round. I know enough to realize that love knows no boundary. Love does not understand tribe or race. Love promotes unity and makes diversity interesting. Love is peace, Mom. Those are some of the roles of love generally. Love does not see Hausa, Yoruba, Igbo, Edo, Ibibio, White, Hispanic or Black like you do, Mom. Love sees humans as humans. But when love specifically becomes romantic like the one Umar and I have for each other, race and tribe are inconsequential."

"You are getting it all wrong, Titi," Kunle informed his daughter.

"Yes, you are getting it all wrong," Biola reaffirmed. "As long as your father and I live, you'll never marry a Hausa boy."

"You didn't even take time to get to know Umar," Titi responded. "You didn't even give him a chance to prove he's the right or the wrong guy for your daughter. You embarrassed and gave him an outright rejection based on his tribe. That's not fair. That's injustice."

"He's just an individual who happens to be of Hausa extraction," Titi continued. "He came into this world just like you and I. Just like everyone else in the world. He didn't ask to be Hausa, just like we didn't ask to be Yorubas. The exact way a white man didn't ask to be white. In the same manner, a black man didn't ask to be black. The same goes for Asians, Hispanics, Latinos, Arabs, and other races, tribes and ethnic groups."

"We all found ourselves here," Titi went on. "That young man in your living room is the most ideal son-in-law any parent could wish for. He treats me well and respects me as a woman. He's not only smart and innovative, he's also a very responsible young man. Above all, he loves me very dearly. Unfortunately, you never troubled to find out all of these things about him. To you, his only shortcoming is his tribal identity. When is being a Hausa become a crime?" Titi asked rhetorically as she stormed out of her parents' bedroom.

She tried to put on a straight face when she got to the living room. She was surprised to find Umar as calm as ever on the same spot she had left him. His demeanor was unbelievable.

"I think we scheduled a wrong time," Titi said after apologizing for her parents' behavior.

"Oh no, sweetheart. There is nothing wrong with our schedule. Come on. I know you are trying to fix this. I know you very well. I should be on my way now, as I wouldn't want my being here to aggravate the already tense situation. Please tell your mom and dad I love them," Umar said as they hugged and headed towards the door.

Titi walked Umar to the gate. Tears dropped from her eyes at every blink. It was unbelievable that they just walked into the house on the same path a few minutes earlier in excitement and now were going back dejected, confused, embarrassed and unsure if they had a future together. The long-awaited meeting halted. Dinner ruined. Efforts wasted. Relationship strained.

Outside the gate, they talked briefly and agreed not to cancel their earlier plan. They had earlier agreed that Titi would meet his father and siblings at the end of the month. Umar would leave Abuja for Kaduna a day prior to Titi's visit. He would drive to the airport to pick up Titi and bring her home to meet his family.

The only consolation for Titi was the promise that Umar made to her that he would tell his father the story of the unpleasant encounter with Titi's parents. He assured Titi that he would arrange a meeting for both parents. The grand plan was to create an opportunity for his father—a liberal-minded gentleman—to broker a peace treaty that would clean up the tribal line drawn by Titi's parents.

Afterwards, they bade each other farewell as Umar opened the front passenger side of the car. He sat comfortably, giving Oliver an impression that whatever it was that brought him to town was over and successful. Titi stood there by the gate and watched as the car drove off. She walked up to the east side wall of the fence after locking the gate behind her. She cried again. This time, she let it all out completely. It was a blood-curdling cry—a full session of it.

CHAPTER 16:

THE FINAL STRAW

For me, I am driven by two main philosophies: know more today about the world than I knew yesterday and lessen the suffering of others. You'd be surprised how far that gets you.

– Neil deGrasse Tyson

The ride back to the hotel was not as interesting as the first lap. Oliver tried to pick up from where they left off. However, he noticed that Umar was not keen at evaluating topics the way he did earlier when he picked him from the hotel. He eventually stopped trying after about three attempts at changing topics with simple no, yes and okay responses from Umar.

Obviously, Umar wasn't a good actor. He couldn't sustain the "everything went well" false impression he had given Oliver earlier. There was an odd silence until they got back to the hotel. Umar thanked Oliver for his service, paid his bill, handed Oliver a good tip and headed straight to his room.

He had an early morning flight back to Abuja the next day. He needed to be at work, so he went to bed early, but unfortunately couldn't sleep. He just couldn't get his mind off what happened at Titi's parents' house. Unlike Titi, Umar had a title for the drama: Tribalism.

Yes, tribalism. He knew enough to treat racism and tribalism as diseases of the mind. "How could Titi's parents wield such an intense prejudice based on tribe even with their superlative college education?" he wondered.

Well, college education is not a cure to such a heart disease in itself. It is a pointer to the cure. College education does not necessarily cure a racist of racism disease or eradicate tribe-inclined sentiments from those who harbor such heinous sentiments. One of the things college education consistently does is provide a strong ability to reason logically.

It's super-amazing to also note that some folks reason logically very well without having a college education. The ability to reason logically changes the game of everyday living. It distinctly shows you, among other things, how and why humans should be assessed, evaluated and dealt with according to their character and not judged on the basis of race or tribe.

As Umar laid there on the bed, he had a deep thought—a really deep thought. He thought about all the preparations that went into what turned out to be an abrupt meeting with Titi's parents. The rehearsals. The flight and hotel reservations. The moments he became a nervous wreck. Those moments he felt like a superman. The excitement. All the great expectations. Only to be allowed to say just two things—"Kaduna" and "yes, ma'am" — and the meeting was over. It was more than absurd.

He added rejection to his mental list of things that are hard to handle, having experienced it first-hand. He finally set the alarm on the night stand and went to sleep. It was such a short night. He woke up before the alarm could go off. He already checked out before his ride arrived. So he was able to beat the Lagos chaotic Monday morning rush-hour traffic and make it on time for his flight.

It was the first domestic flight out of Lagos Murtala Muhammed Airport. The flight to Abuja was a smooth one. As the plane taxied to the gate, he was delighted that his luggage was a carry-on. He didn't have to waste time at the baggage claim area. He only needed to get to his car in the airport parking lot, pay his parking fees and drive straight to the office.

The day went by so fast, and so did the entire week. Before he knew it, it was already the end of the month. Titi would be arriving in Kaduna from Lagos the next day to meet his father and his siblings. Umar was already in Kaduna. The youngest of the siblings had teased Umar all day. He noticed the excitement in everything Umar did and attributed it to Titi's planned visit. They laughed heartily about it. That translated to the fact that Umar's brother was right in his assertion.

That night was one of the longest for Umar. The next day was going to be memorable. He had two important tasks to accomplish. The first was to introduce Titi to the Rufai family. The second was to notify his father of Titi's parents' rejection of him and get him to commit to a peace-making initiative geared towards resolving the issue.

Minutes rolled into hours and it was morning already. The long-awaited day had arrived—a day he would take an important step toward becoming a family man. His father had invited one of his close friends, Rimi Abubakar. Everyone in the Rufai Family knew Rimi. He had been friends with Aliu, Umar's father, for a very long time. They grew up together. Aliu invited Rimi over to be part of the excitement—the informal introduction of Umar's fiancée to the family.

Titi was scheduled to arrive at 9:45 in the morning. The weather was good. There was no expectation of flight cancelation. The airport was about a 45-minute drive from the Rufai residence. Umar left home around 7:15 in the morning in one of the cars in the compound—a Peugeot 505 Evolution – Limited Series. His father bought him the car brand new as a graduation gift. Surprisingly, Umar brought the car back to Kaduna from Abuja as soon as he bought his own car with his own money. Aliu was not surprised, though. He knew his son was very independent.

Umar got to the airport super-early and had to wait for Titi's arrival. He didn't mind the long wait. To him, it was a lot better than being late and forced to drive crazy. For close to two hours, he waited patiently in the arrival lounge. It was a great expectation. He looked steadily at the long, wide walkway filled with arriving passengers coming out from different gates.

Around 9:38, he began to imagine the aircraft boarded by Titi taxi towards one of the gates from the runway. As he began to visualize Titi's excitement, the drive back home and ultimately, the introduction of Titi to his father and siblings, he spotted her walking from across the wide walkway. At this time, Umar was sitting on one of the high chairs at the arrival lounge. The chair was more like a bar stool. It was high enough to see arriving passengers as they walked out from the gates and headed towards the baggage claim area.

Titi stopped momentarily to look around. She was obviously looking to see if she could catch a glimpse of Umar somewhere trying to locate her. Umar took in every moment. He tried as hard as he could to suppress the urge to leap from the high chair. He liked what he saw and took his time to admire Titi's beauty before emerging from the lounge to let her know he was as punctual as ever.

Titi was such a beauty to behold. Her unique walk was angelic. She had on a simple chiffon dress that looked more like Rayon. The dress wasn't too clingy or *décolleté* in any sense of those words. It wasn't too conservative, either. One really had to take a second look to realize it was not a jumpsuit. It was simple but very elegant.

It was a semi-button-down with a wrap-like design on the upper front side. The lower part had an A-line skirt design and fitted closely around the waist. Each time she took a step, the slight wider bottom of the dress swiped the stylishly handcrafted shoes she had on. They were fancy black sling-back shoes with leather lining and adjustable buckles that she bought specifically for the trip—a trip to meet her prospective father-in-law.

Everything Titi had on, from the trendy neck-hugging braids hairdo to the triangle heel sling-back shoes, conferred on her a perfect blend of full sparkle and a classic princess look. She didn't have to go to the baggage claim area as she had just a carry-on suitcase. She stopped again and looked around hoping to see Umar around—somewhere.

However, it didn't really seem like Umar was done admiring her. He kept watching as Titi walked farther away from the lounge. "God must have spent extra time creating this lady. She's beautiful on the outside and much more beautiful on the inside," he said to himself as he finally got up from the high chair.

If there was anything Titi knew about Umar, it was his punctuality. Aside from being independent, selfless and kind-hearted, Umar never showed up late for anything. He planned ahead of time. Just as she began to wonder why he was not at the airport yet, Umar walked up to her from behind. "Is there someone you are looking for?" He asked Titi in a disguised voice.

As soon as she turned around to answer the question and discovered it was Umar, she let go of the carry-on and jumped in his arms.

"Humm! You are late for the first time," Titi said after they were done hugging each other.

"Nope! I'm not late," Umar defended himself. "I've been watching you from the moment you walked out from the gate area."

"What was that for?" Titi queried.

"When did it become a crime for a man to admire his wife-to-be?" he asked, making a funny face.

"You are so silly," she commented.

"Well, I'm silly for a good reason," Umar responded.

They both laughed hysterically as Umar showed her the way to the parking lot. He told her how gorgeous she looked and how proud he was to finally have an opportunity to introduce her to his father and siblings. In that short distance between the terminal and the parking lot, they switched from topic to topic. He couldn't stop expressing his admiration of Titi's dress. He knew she had a penchant for fashion just like him, and he never missed or skipped complimenting her.

As they drove home, they also, among other things, discussed the flight, preparations for the meeting and the task ahead—disclosing Titi's parents' rejection of him based on tribe and convincing his father to commit to meeting Titi's parents and brokering a peace treaty.

They finally got home. As the car pulled up by the gate, one of Aliu's domestic workers opened the gate. Titi was not in any way prepared for what he saw. It was a gigantic mansion of a sort compared to what she expected. As soon as they drove in, Umar got out of the car, went around it to the passenger side and opened the door for Titi.

"Thank you," she said as she looked everywhere. "It's a beautiful house. Now I know where you got the good taste from. Your dad sure has some good taste."

"Thank you," Umar responded.

He held her hand as they walked from a detached garage where the Peugeot 505 Evolution was parked. It was one of several detached garages in the compound. They held hands with their fingers intertwined as they headed towards the main building. Umar ushered her through well-designed interlocking paths that bordered a beautiful spread-out lawn.

It was a vast lawn. Titi found it alluring. She tilted her head as her eyes searched for the end of the lawn. She noticed a paved patio at the west end of the building where the lawn ended. The patio had a combination of stylish hip and gable roof. It was intentionally designed to be impervious to any precipitation.

At the end of the interlocking path, they made a left turn to a neatly paved walkway that led into the building. Once inside, Umar ushered her into the main living room. From the guest waiting area to the main living room, Titi noticed all the classic interior décors and stylish fittings. As meticulous as she was, nothing came across as being short of a combination of stately trend and modern style.

Umar's siblings already converged in the living room. One of them had caught a glimpse of the August visitor at the time they drove in and had informed the others. He had also humorously told them to be on their best behavior. One after the other, Umar introduced them. They all seemed to like Titi instantly. They smiled broadly. There was an undisputable expression of satisfaction on everyone's countenance.

"Where is dad?" Umar asked as he turned to no one in particular.

"In the courtyard with Mr. Abubakar," the youngest volunteered.

Umar's siblings all disappeared from the living room after exchanging pleasantries with Titi. They had a grand plan—to reappear at the time their father would be meeting Titi. They wouldn't miss that moment for anything. As soon as they left, Umar made a gesture with his right hand to Titi, asking her to sit. Their hands disengaged for the first time since they got back from the airport as Titi sat comfortably on the couch.

"Give me a minute, please. I need to let dad know you are here," he told her as he left the living room for the courtyard area.

Titi could tell that Umar was super excited. She sat there alone. For the first time since she walked into the house, her heart skipped a beat. She couldn't explain why that happened. She was confident that she dressed responsibly. "Maybe it's a natural thing," she consoled herself.

She had seen Umar's father's pictures in his photograph collections on campus. The only thing she knew from the pictures was that the man had an intimidating physique. With just a few minutes inside the house, she had seen more pictures and life portraits of him on the wall and by the wall and the intimidation played out some more. She knew nothing about his personality, though Umar had told her several times that he was an orator.

She began to build confidence in herself before the man walked in. She needed that confidence to restore a normal heartbeat. She knew in her heart that she would get along with Umar's dad. With her pedigree—well-nurtured young lady, a devout Christian, graduating student with the best results in the school. These were some of the excellent qualities Umar said he had shared with his father about her. With a modest pride, she felt every grown man would do anything to have her as a daughter-in-law.

Just as she began to build her confidence back up, Umar entered the living room. This time, he was not alone. On his heels was his father with Rimi, his childhood friend, who everyone in the household referred to as Mr. Abubakar. Umar's siblings also followed them as they had earlier planned. Before Umar could say a word, his father broke the silence. "How are you, young lady?" Aliu asked, stretching forth his right hand to Titi for a handshake.

Titi was a little confused. She and Umar never rehearsed this part. In Nigeria, the Yoruba people train their kids to be respectful, especially to people who are older. It is considered disrespectful to have a handshake with older adults. If you must have a handshake with an older person, the older folk should be the one initiating it. As a young lady, you'll have to go down on your knees to receive such a handshake. As a young man, you'll have to either prostrate or at the least, bow your head as a sign of respect and honor while receiving the handshake.

For the Hausa folks, she wasn't too sure. In her mind, she felt she should have researched the Hausa way of handling such a situation. She had no time to think it through. Aliu already stretched forth his hand. He planned to introduce her to Rimi and the rest of the kids himself. "I'm doing okay. Thank you, sir," Titi responded as she accepted the handshake on a bended knee.

She felt that was the best she could do in that situation. She wanted to crisscross cultures and at least meet the Hausa culture half-way. So she felt accepting Aliu's handshake on a bended knee cut across all cultures in Nigeria. However, Aliu didn't seem to have any issue with the way the knee went—straight, bent, full or all the way down.

"You are so pretty. So you're the mystery girl who stole my son's large heart," he joked.

"What's your name?" He realized all of a sudden that he never asked Umar Titi's name.

"My name is Titilola," Titi responded as she continued to build more confidence.

"Teetee-lau-lau," Aliu repeated, trying to grasp the right pronunciation.

"Titilola, sir," Titi tried correcting him courteously. "You can call me Titi. That's what family and friends call me," she added.

"Don't tell me you are a Yoruba girl?" retorted Aliu.

"Yes sir. I'm a Yoruba girl. My parents are originally from Idanre in Ondo State, but I was born and brought up in Lagos," Titi responded.

The discovery that Titi was a Yoruba girl didn't go down well with Aliu. His countenance changed instantly. There was an uncomfortable long silence. At that moment, a pin drop would have made a deafening sound. Aliu's children had never seen him with such a scary facial expression. He removed his hat and turned to Rimi. "This is more than terrible" was the expression on Rimi's face. And within the blink of an eye, the expression changed to "How could Umar do this?"

The scenario was reminiscent of a traditional moment of silence observed in respect for a departed soul. Everyone was embarrassed and confused, except Aliu and Rimi, who were both stunned at the same time. Eventually, Aliu broke the silence as he turned to Umar. "We obviously need to talk…and we need to do it right now," Aliu fumed as he turned and walked towards his bedroom.

Umar hesitated. He needed some time to process what just happened. He needed to be sure it was his father—a love crusader—was the same man who displayed what he just witnessed. He stood there motionless trying to take it all in. He knew he had to do something. Not only did he have to do something, he had to do it fast.

His fiancée was right there waiting on him to see how he would handle the ugly situation. His siblings were waiting to see what he would do next. Rimi's eyes were all over him. Ironically, Rimi was the least of his concerns. His body language already showed his position—prejudice against his intentions to marry a Yoruba girl. To an extent, Rimi had an influence on Aliu. Umar would have asked him to come with him to his father's room just so he could lend a helping hand while trying to obtain his father's blessings on his relationship with Titi.

With Rimi eliminated as a possible help, Umar turned to Titi. He noticed her tear-filled eyes. At that point he tried all he could to conceal his, but a blink was all it took for both of them. The tears dropped uncontrollably and they both sobbed like babies. Afterwards, Umar pulled himself together, realizing he still needed to be strong for Titi. He whispered some incoherent words into Titi's ears and headed towards his father's bedroom. The moment he entered the room, he needed no one to tell him Aliu was still angry. He shivered profusely. He ranted and then ranted.

"What came over you, Umar? Why did you decide to make me unhappy after all I've done for you guys? Through thick and thin, I took care of all of you since your mom's untimely death. And all you could pay me back with is coming home with a Yoruba girl? What gives you an impression that it's okay to want to spend the rest of your life with a Yoruba girl? Has the world suddenly run out of Hausa girls? I'm so disappointed in you. You are an embarrassment. You are..."

"Really, dad," Umar cut in. "Is this really you? You are acting like I committed a murder. Your action is at variance with the love crusade everyone knows you for. It is at variance with the values of Christianity that you brought us up with. All the years I was in the university, I lived by those values. I performed excellently well in my academics. I never joined gangs of law-breakers. I never did drugs. I never made you lose sleep. I never discriminated against anyone like you've always told us not to. And now, you are furious that I brought home someone I feel would make me happy for the rest of my life just because of her tribe? Dad, I should be the one disappointed in you."

"How dare you talk to me in such a manner?" Aliu fired back. "I can see she has been a bad influence on you. As your dad, all I ask of you is to end this relationship and find yourself a Hausa girl. Deal, or no deal?" He asked his signature question after every discussion.

"No deal. Absolutely no deal on this one, dad," Umar insisted.

It was the first time Aliu heard his son give him an emphatic "no deal" response. At that point, it began to dawn on him that attempting to make Umar change his mind would be a herculean task. He knew he had to adopt a different strategy, as it was obvious to him that instilling fear in his son's mind through confrontation wasn't going to produce the desired result.

On a good day, Umar was not argumentative. It was a surprise for Aliu that his son assumed a different role defending his Yoruba princess. The emergency meeting he summoned his son for was supposed to be a discussion, but it ended up as a heated argument session between father and son. Deep in his heart, Aliu knew his son was right on every point he raised, but pride and his animosity for people outside of his tribe wouldn't let him reason the right way.

Umar was overwhelmed and physically exhausted. He thought about his promises to Titi on having his father talk to her parents. He thought about how he had relied so much on his father's expected intervention. But now, his father turned out worse than Titi's parents. He never saw that coming, not from his dear dad.

With no deal reached, Umar stormed out of his father's bedroom. He was more like a lifeless being. Titi was all alone in the living room with a very gloomy look when he got there. As soon as Titi saw him, she knew instantly that all didn't go well between father and son. In tears, Umar offered some incoherent explanation.

They eventually called the airline to see if there was any flight to Lagos later that evening. They had to drive back to the airport, having discovered the last Lagos-bound flight was on a late evening schedule. They could only hope the flight was not fully booked.

Umar made several attempts to stop by at some restaurants for her to have a meal before flying out, but Titi insisted she was okay. Obviously, she lost her appetite for food. She had paled at the thought of all that was going on. She went from gloomy to dejected.

At the airport, they went straight to the airline ticketing area. Once a seat was confirmed for Titi, Umar paid for the cost of the ticket change. They spent a few minutes preceding departure discussing what their next line of action would be. They didn't have the luxury of time. There were just a few minutes before departure and they couldn't come up with a plan.

Obviously, they were too emotional to rush each other into making a decision. They both agreed the situation was a clog in the wheel of progress of their relationship. It was a huge mess, which required a reasonable amount of clean up time. Umar promised to call her on her parents' home phone for further discussion as Titi headed towards the departure gates.

As she flew back to Lagos, she became confused and disturbed at the same time. As agitated as she was, she wondered how her tribe nullified all of her good qualities—the attributes she had worked so hard for all her life. To her, all her accolades had gone down the drain because of her "Yoruba girl" identity.

The more she thought about it, the more aggrieved she became. She wondered why people would not treat people as humans rather than based on race or tribe. "Why would my tribe define me and not my character? Why would my tribe describe me and not my personality? Why would my tribe be an attestation of who I am and not my attributes? Why should I be judged by my tribe and not by the content of my character? It's such a cruel world we live in," she concluded.

CHAPTER 17:

HEINOUS STRATEGY

Love and compassion are necessities, not luxuries. Without
them, humanity cannot survive.

– Dalai Lama XIV

Umar's heart bled as Titi walked towards the departure gates. He could only hope his dreams of spending the rest of his life with her did not crumble like a pack of cards. Then, his heart bled some more. He fought so hard to control the tears as his eyes became tear-filled. He lost the fight. Then, the tears dropped. The first drop rolled down his cheek and the second drop followed in a quick succession. He just let the tears all out as he could no longer control them. Both sides of his face below the eyes soon became moist from the tears.

Eventually, he reached out for a piece of handkerchief in the right front pocket of his pants and wiped his face. He thought about their both parents as he attempted to keep his face dry with the white hanky. He thought of how Titi's parents and his father were divided by tribe and united by tribalism.

In his mind, he felt it was a serious issue for the human race that people's diversity, in term of race, culture, custom, tradition and language—which should have been potent sources of unity and strength—was now a tool utilized to wield bitterness, hate, bigotry and discrimination. He then began to ask himself questions endlessly. Why do we curtail love? Why do we impede love's determined attempts to illuminate the world? Why don't we allow love to flow endlessly?

He had not taken a step since Titi walked through the security checks. He hoped the bitter story would have changed to a sweet one the next time they met. He hoped that their parents' self-inflicted wounds of tribalism would heal over time.

He was wrong—the wounds never healed. Unfortunately, it was the last time he ever saw Titi. No, the plane didn't crash, but their hopes did. The affection did not die, but another chance to see Titi did.

Like a puppet waiting to be animated by the voice of a ventriloquist, Umar stood still for a long time and then sluggishly walked away to the parking lot. He had a hard time locating where he parked the car. He was at the right parking zone but in the wrong lane. He had so much going on in his mind that he didn't notice he had walked past his car twice.

He searched frantically from lane to lane. At some point, he stopped momentarily and then proceeded with his sluggish walk as he walked past the car the third time. This time, the car was right within his view. Funny enough, he still couldn't see it. All he could see was a very thick dark cloud of misery that hovered over his engagement to Titi.

At this time, Umar knew something was not right with him. It looked more like he had suddenly become a victim of emotional stress so quickly. Titi's rejection by his father had a devastating effect on his ability to think. He then leaned back to grab a steel pole by the curb. It appeared his foot could no longer support his body weight, so he slightly let go of the pole, dropped his entire body at the base of the pole. With the pole behind his back, he slanted a little bit to make an incline with his back as he rested his upper body around the neck region against the pole.

It was the most uncomfortable posture. However, he felt better compared to being on his feet. He was right on the verge of passing out before he settled for the uncomfortable posture. He has had a significant drop of oxygen flow to the brain. His state of confusion had transitioned to blurred vision. By the time the blurred vision cleared, he realized he was sitting on a bare floor.

It was a brief episode of unconsciousness. As he got up, it took him a couple of seconds to realize where he was—the airport parking lot. He soon connected the dots and became aware of the fact that he just had a momentary blackout. He looked around to see if someone was watching. He then dusted off his sleeves with his right palm.

Afterwards, he walked one lane over to where his car was parked. He didn't miss it this time, as the car was still clearly within his view. As he drove out of the parking lot, he was more than convinced that whatever it was he experienced before he grabbed the steel pole was precipitated by cognitive dissonance.

As he drove home, he made a conscious effort to be alert behind the wheel. At 65 miles per hour, he needed no one to remind him of how disastrous it would be if he didn't pay attention, lost concentration and eventually lost control of the car. As soon as he got back home, he went straight to his room and locked the door behind him. He contemplated going to see his father in his bedroom. The plan was to let his dad know of the near-death experience he had at the airport to see if that would evoke some kind of empathy from him. However, he talked himself out of such move.

He had a different plan. He left for Abuja the next morning. He left without a farewell to his dad. Obviously, he was still angry with him for what he described as Titi's unexpected loathsome treatment. For him, the treatment was not only reprehensible and despicable, but it was inhumane in every sense of the word. Umar was raised not to bear grudges. Unfortunately, at this time, nothing else mattered to him. Not even any of the good traits he imbibed growing up with his dad.

His argument was that if his dad, who instilled in him all the good manners in the world, with all the good values the Christian faith could offer, could break the rule of love by making it conditional and attaching tribal sentiment to human acceptance, he felt justified to bear a grudge against him.

However, he knew deep inside him that the teachings from the Bible do not support bearing grudges no matter what, but he was just too torn apart by his dad's disappointing behavior. At the same time, he was guilt-ridden having to leave without a farewell to his dad.

Umar quickly settled down at his job in Abuja. He tried all he could to put everything behind him. As hard as he tried, there was one thing he couldn't place on the back burner—Titi. He thought about her every now and then. He could no longer reach her. She could no longer reach him.

It was a crossroad of a sort for Umar. He began to drift away from his known enviable record of high productivity level at work. There were dents all over his emotions. In the most aggressive manner, the dents became more and more visible. His innovative attributes disappeared.

Gradually, the quality of his services began to drop. At some point, the services were no longer commensurate with his remuneration.

Everything seemed to have headed south for Umar. His manager noticed and called his attention to the ugly situation a couple of times.

Titi's parents were more than determined to make sure Titi and Umar didn't work. Not under their watch. They knew there was no way for them to keep a twenty-four-hour watch over Titi. So their first strategy was to inhibit communication between Titi and Umar in the best way they could. Kunle and Biola both agreed to change the home phone number. To make this happen, they took a day off and drove to the area office of Nigerian Telecommunications Limited. NITEL, as the telecoms company was popularly referred to at the time, was a telephone service company in Nigeria. The company had a monopoly of the telecommunications industry, being a sole player in that massive sector of the economy.

As expected, NITEL had a field day—maybe a field century— until 1992, when the telecommunications sector was deregulated. The Nigerian government, under military rule at the time, enacted what was known as Nigerian Communications Commission Act, which launched an array of innovative players in the nation's telecom sector. It was a below-the-belt blow for NITEL. Not only was its age-long monopoly broken, but it struggled to keep up with the attendant marketplace competition that came with the demise of the monopoly.

Before then, a home phone was not just a mode of communication, but owning one was a luxury as well as a status symbol of sorts. Applying for a home phone or requesting a change of number was more like applying for a mortgage. The application was complicated, the paperwork was cumbersome and the approval process was stringent.

But then, Kunle and Biola were more than ready to go through the stress—anything that would keep Titi, their lovely Yoruba girl, away from Umar, the detested Hausa boy, was no stress for them. As a matter of fact, the process of acquiring a new home phone number was a lot quicker than expected for them. Biola knew how to play the "who knows who" card very well. She would pass for a grand master in the game. She understood the rules way beyond an average player.

Some of NITEL's directors, who knew how to brandish artificial line scarcity in the face of home phone applicants, were customers at the bank where Biola was a Corporate Communications Director. A few of these directors needed to have their transactions at the bank processed with lightning speed—from new accounts to wire transfers and everything in between.

Biola had no issue instructing customer-facing associates to make speed and skip-the-queue happen. So she basically pressed the "Return Favor" button when her household needed a new home phone number. A bizarre case of rub my back and I'll rub yours.

Biola's "who knows who" card eventually paid off. One of the directors at NITEL who patronized her bank literally followed the application up. He made sure every team that had to work on the home telephone line request did so expediently.

The request got an approval in no time. Titi's parents' home phone number was swapped and the old number recycled accordingly. As the NITEL technician who did the installation left Titi's parents' property, so did the communication between Titi and Umar. At the time—with no cell phones, no home address, no social media—loss of contact was very easy.

On his part, Aliu took a different approach in an attempt to halt communication between Umar and Titi. His approach was a more heinous strategy. Aside changing his own home phone number just like Titi's parents, Aliu, through his influential and powerful politician friends, was able to schedule a meeting with the chairman of the board of directors of the company Umar worked for in Abuja.

The main item on the meeting agenda was friendly fire—a layoff in the nation's corporate world with a specific employee as a target. In this case, the purpose was to have Umar fired from the company just so he could relocate back to Kaduna and accept one of the numerous job offers orchestrated by his father.

The chairman of the Board of Directors swung into action after the meeting. With the caliber of politicians who initiated the ad-hoc meeting, he knew that obliging such request would place the company on the favor list of government's *juicy* contracts. He put a call across to the CEO expressing interest in a specific employee—Umar Rufai.

Subsequently, when the CEO summoned Umar's manager, the company's Director of Research and Development, he knew something wasn't right. How on earth would the CEO be personally interested in a Junior Engineer's appraisal? He smelled a friendly fire immediately. However, he couldn't discuss what he suspected with Umar, when he was eventually fired.

Umar, on his part, didn't suspect any foul play. He concluded in his mind that his being laid off had to do with the recent decline in the quality of his performance at work. Of course, at one point, his boss called his attention to this. He knew it was a result of the emotional turmoil he'd been subjected to because of the potential threats to his engagement to Titi, but unfortunately, he couldn't figure a way around the instability that surrounded his emotions.

After losing his job, Umar found himself in the labor market again. Reluctantly, he updated his resume and began to hope for another opportunity. Days rolled into months with no invitation for interviews, let alone a job offer. Then, he began to run low on his savings. His bills began to accumulate.

Now, he had just one month before his annual rent expired. With no income for several months, Umar began to look for alternatives. For the first time, he experienced what life toughness was about. He tried unsuccessfully to call Titi several times. His theory was that hearing Titi's voice would do much to ameliorate his battered emotions. For him, it was a double blow: dealing with all the issues that arose from his job loss and being completely cut off from the love of his life.

In the middle of this, he received a message from his dad. He wanted him to consider one of the job offers in Kaduna. These were jobs he could get on a golden platter with or without an interview. Aliu was that influential.

Ironically, these were the same jobs he turned down earlier as a fresh graduate. But the bait was too enticing this time. With debts piling up in the face of uncertainty, an unexpected job loss in the middle of emotional and psychological torture, no source of income and the tormenting reality of the communication breakdown with Titi, bouts of unpleasant events and a looming state of depression, the bait of a job offer with his dad as a source was simply irresistible.

Eventually, he swallowed his pride, against his wishes, and accepted one of the job offers after a week-long evaluation. Then, he moved back to Kaduna afterwards. For him, moving back to Kaduna came with a string of challenges. None of the offers came with an offer of accommodation—an indication that he would have to move in with his dad, at least initially.

The arrangement, no doubt, had a dent on his relationship with his dad. He began to suspect his dad as the evil genius behind his sudden job loss. He had read about friendly fire in the nation's corporate world in one of the general classes in his college days. Unfortunately, he had no evidence to nail Aliu with. It was a "what if it was him, what if it was not him" kind of situation.

CHAPTER 18:

GOODBYE TOMORROW

*Courage. Kindness. Friendship. Character. These are the
qualities that define us as human beings, and propel us,
on occasion, to greatness.*

– R.J. Palacio

Twenty-three years have passed since Umar and Titi lost contact.
How time flies! Titi has always reminisced about their last time
together at the Kaduna Airport. She still remembers virtually everything. All the details of every event that unfolded on the fateful last
day together. She remembers it all. Very vividly, too.

Every detail: the confusion, the profuse tears, the inability to
come up with a "next plan" strategy as a result of their states of mind,
the last hug, the long walk to the departure gates and her miserable
feelings aboard her flight back to Lagos.

A string of questions still haunts her. Where is Umar? Where,
on earth, could he be? Did he change his mind about her on that
fateful last day? Did Umar's dad come up with a reason good enough
to convince him to abandon her? What exactly happened?

These and many more were the constant questions in the list
for Titi. It is a general belief anywhere in the world that time heals

wounds. However, for Titi, time had failed to perform one of its basic responsibilities. It didn't seem like time had bothered to do anything to heal her wounds over the years—more than two decades now. Every time she tries to let the whole misery slip from her mind, she would sigh woefully and blab incoherently to herself.

She seemed to always have an inordinate desire to unravel the mystery and at least have closure. The more she tried, the more miserable she became. It challenged her imagination that her case had become an exception for the healing power of time.

Twenty-three years gone by. A lot of events had unfolded in those years, locally and around the globe. History was made at some points as well as unexpected development in many facets of life. The expected had ceased numerous times. Climate had changed. Tensions, chaos and disorders had culminated in wars after wars at different times. Peace treaties had been brokered on different occasions. A durable ceasefire and a sustainable truce had been reached as well. Numerous events had indeed unfolded within the twenty-three years.

But then, there was one thing that stood out in all the events that characterized the last two decades and three years: technology. Technology has evolved in a way and manner that transcended human understanding. It began its journey into our world as a "magical" science or craft and has since blown everyone's mind with its unbelievable evolvement into artificial intelligence. Frequency Division Multiple Access (FDMA), Time Division Multiple Access (TDMA) and Code Division Multiple Access (CDMA) technologies have all revolutionized the telecommunication industry, making mobile phones usage a possibility.

It's now more like a fairy tale to realize that computer chips are more like human brains, Ultra Short Throw 4K Projectors are possibly going to be the future of television and Hover Boards are already a reality, Google's smart contact lenses are deployed to monitor blood sugar levels, nanotechnology is not resting on its oars and just when you think the world has seen it all in the world of technology, Silicon Valley rolls out another piece of wonder aimed at making life and living a lot more comfortable. What more could humanity ask for?

The evolution of technology has not only left us with amazing methods and concise ways of task accomplishment in everyday living, but it has also presented a new academic discipline; redesigned production techniques—leading to an unprecedented improvement in productivity; improved precision in forecasting; and literally impacted all spheres of human endeavor: economy, finance, accounting, surveillance, security, construction, human, capital and natural resources management, logistics, aviation, entertainment, childcare, healthcare—everything.

Technology is more like the proverbial water. Water is an all-time essential. You can't do without it. So is technology. One of technology's byproducts is social media. With social media, digital platforms are provided for social networking with an awesome ability to share contents endlessly. These social media became some kind of craze that spread like wildfire. Everyone hops on it, reconnects with old friends and makes new friends as well.

Titi was not left out in the craze. She hopped onto a couple of social media. Unlike a considerable number of people on social media platforms, Titi had a specific mission. Her self-imposed task was to search for and connect with Umar. She had used a couple of search engines in the past, but unfortunately, no promising leads came up. So she decided to give social media a shot. Every time she typed in Umar Rufai, she would feel a cold sweat as the results of her search returned. She would drag the mouse and then let it go in a manner reminiscent of touching a hot stove.

The sensory receptors in her skin from the right shoulder blade region would send a sensation in the form of stimuli via nerve fibers to her brainstem and spinal cord. Her fingers would shiver uncontrollably as she clicked on every name identical to Umar's. She would scroll down, up, down, and up again and again with no leads.

Several times, she randomly sent a friend request to some stranger—any random guy with "Rufai" as a last name. Whenever her friend requests were accepted, her first message to these individuals was always "Are you, by chance, related to one Umar Rufai who graduated from Ahmadu Bello University?" This became a tradition for her; but no one seemed to know this Umar Rufai each time she asked.

The misery deepened, with no solution. The searches yielded no results. The more aggressive she became, the more elusive Umar got. It had been twenty-three years and counting. She had obviously not moved on with her life at all. Not even an inch. She was always buried in confusion. She couldn't find an appropriate name for what she contended with—tough love or what? Was it an inability to let go?

For the most part, she blamed herself. She feels she shouldn't have left Kaduna that fateful day—the day that went down as their last day together. She has always been of an opinion that if she had checked in to a hotel that night, instead of the change of return ticket option she went for, Umar wouldn't have left her at the hotel alone.

She strongly feels they would have spent the night together and that would have afforded them an opportunity of time—all the time needed to agree on a next-step strategy for their relationship. Instead, they both made a costly mistake—she thinks. She'll blink and let off the piled up tears. As the tears drop, she'll give a low moan of despair and engage the closest object to her in some kind of fist battle. She'll then wonder how and why they allowed the turbulence of tribalism to blow away a rare unconditional love?

One day, the last Saturday in the month of September, Titi decided to spend the entire day indoors. It was a sunny afternoon. Earlier in the mid-morning, she had peeped through the blinds to see if the sunrise would tarry just so she could predict what the moisture in the air would be like for the day. She looked towards the sky for a trace of clouds. She had very particular meteorological phenomena to forecast the day's weather from.

For her, the amount of clouds in the sky at a certain period of time in the mid-morning determined how the rest of the day turned out to be in term of weather. Inside a scanty amount of clouds usually lurks the prospect for a sunny day. She loves the indoors and would do anything to stay in and enjoy the comfort that the privacy of her home offers her. One would assume that a sunny day was enough of a reason to be outdoors—not for Titi.

She had just raised her head from her home-office desk. A surge in her blood pressure jolted her back to life from her once-in-a-while Umar-induced trance. She then decided to login to her Facebook account before going to the kitchen to put something together for lunch. As she browsed through some posted updates, a pop-up notification caught her attention. Out of curiosity, she clicked and discovered it was a friend request from some random guy. She couldn't ignore the request for an obvious reason: The random guy's name was Aminu Rufai. With a Rufai last name, Titi was all in for a confirmation. She didn't see a need to check out the guy's profile before confirming and by default added him to her contact list. "Anything for a Rufai last name," she enthused.

A closer look at the random guy's profile picture didn't trigger any memory. Then, she navigated to the messaging tab to send her signature message. As soon as she typed, "Are you, by chance, related to one Umar Rufai who graduated from Ahmadu Bello University?" she noticed the random guy already beat her to it. He had instantaneously sent her a message following the confirmation of the friend request. Titi cleared off her intended message to read the random guy's message.

"Hi" was all she saw in her inbox.

"Hello," she replied.

"Thanks for accepting a friend request from me."

"The pleasure is mine," Titi responded, as she was trying to re-type her signature question.

"My name is Aminu—Aminu Rufai. Are you Titi Olofin, who graduated from Ahmadu Bello University?"

"Yes," Titi replied, clearing off her typed-out signature question from the chat room's message window.

She was curious to know who this guy was. Could this be the beginning of a big break in the mystery surrounding Umar's age-long silence? Is he related to Umar? Would he divulge Umar's whereabouts? A total of a million questions arose in Titi's vivid imagination. She became anxious, uneasy, perturbed and worried—all at the same time.

Then, there was a silence on the other end, a two-minute "no activity" silence. Titi wanted to break the silence so bad. For a minute, she struggled with a decision to type "Are you still there?" Just before she made up her mind, Aminu's message crawled into her side of the chat room.

"Apologies. I was distracted a little bit by a string of text messages I just received."

"That's okay," Titi responded.

"Wow! I thought as much. The moment I saw your face—that pretty face—I knew it was you."

"Wait a minute. Have me met?" Titi queried.

"Oh yes. Over twenty years ago. I'm Aminu. Umar's brother."

The introduction was like no other. Titi didn't know how to process what she just read. Umar's brother? Are you kidding me right now? She started to talk aloud to herself. She just couldn't believe she had Umar's brother at the other end of the chat room. It was a mixed feeling for her—a feeling of excitement and confusion. All of a sudden, the name and face clicked. She remembered how Umar would talk about Aminu as his favorite sibling when they were in college. She also remembered seeing Aminu's pictures in Umar's collections as well as meeting him along with Umar's other siblings.

Finally, there couldn't have been a better person to connect all the dots and provide the missing links—a twenty-three-year missing link. She was just all over the place in her own world of imagination that appeared more like a trance. By the time she stepped out of her imagination and hopped back into the chat room, a total of four messages from Aminu were already waiting.

"Hi. Hello, Titi. Are you still there? Is everything okay?"

"Everything is okay," Titi finally broke the silence.

"It was just like yesterday when my brother brought you home. We all still talk about it."

"Really?"

"Yes. Almost all the time."

"It's been the same way for me. I think about your brother all the time. I must give it to you, though. You have an amazing memory for faces," Titi complimented.

"Thanks," Aminu responded.

"So, tell me. Where is he now?" Titi requested with an eagerness to know where Umar was.

"He's no longer here," Aminu replied.

"I didn't get that. He's no longer here? Here—like where?"

"We lost Umar. He died."

"Died? Umar is dead? How? When? Where? What happened? Umar is dead? Died? Dead?"

"Yes, he died. His wife killed him. It's a long story—so long a story. Too long to type."

"Oh my goodness!"

At this time, Titi began to shiver. Images of Umar began to flash through her mind. She cried like a baby. So much that her eyes were swollen.

Aminu could only imagine her sobbing or wailing on the other side of the chat room. All he could send was, "That's okay. We knew all along that you didn't hear about the tragic event," Aminu said as he tried to console Titi. They eventually exchanged telephone numbers with an agreement to continue the conversation by phone.

Obviously, Titi couldn't wait to call Aminu. But first she had to call Lara, her closest friend, who lived in the same neighborhood, to see if she could come over to her house. She knew she couldn't go to the kitchen again as earlier planned. She lost her appetite for food and needed some company. Once Lara promised she would come later in the day, Titi wiped her tears with her bare hand as she headed to the bedroom for a box of tissues. She buried herself in a sleeper sofa by the side of her bed and painfully let out the tears. When she was all done—at least for that moment—she sluggishly walked back to the PC desk in the home-office area, added Aminu's phone number to the contact list on her phone and placed a call.

"Hello!" Aminu's voice pierced through the phone's mouthpiece.

"Hello, Aminu. It's Titi."

"I do hope you're not hurting too bad with the horrible news. I didn't mean to make the day devastating for you."

"Aminu, did you just say devastating? I've been living a devastating life from the day your dad rejected me based on my tribe. It was the last day I set my eyes on Umar, the man I loved unconditionally. And years after, I'm still a shadow of my former self."

"Umar tried all he could to locate you. He called your parents' phone number numerous times unsuccessfully..."

"I thought as much," Titi cut in. "My parents changed the home telephone number." She told Aminu how she flew to Abuja knowing fully well that Umar must have been making frantic efforts to reach her only to be told that Umar no longer worked for the company he was with at the time.

Aminu promised to compress the story as much as he could. He informed Titi how he personally advised Umar to push everything about her behind him when he discovered that his brother had become an emotional wreck as a result of the daunting tribe-induced challenges that contended with their relationship. He recalled perfectly well that his brother's response was always, "Titi is not an everyday lady who one could forget so easily. I love her with all my heart."

"Dad is such an evil genius," Aminu submitted. He informed Titi how their dad orchestrated a "friendly fire" that cost Umar his job in

Abuja just so he could be at dad's beck and call. He knew Umar had a very strong will and a mind of his own. So his mission was to make him subservient. With time, he succeeded after making Umar lose his job. He organized another job for him in Kaduna and eventually set him up with a match-making gimmick with Halima, the daughter of one of his top politician friends. Umar eventually succumbed after a few years of frustration and several bouts of suffocating pressure from dad.

"Halima is a Hausa girl. Right?" Titi asked, trying to make sense of Umar's dad's plan as well as confirm Halima's tribal identity.

"Yes, she's Hausa," Aminu confirmed. He added that Halima was the daughter of Alhaji Abubakar Shuaib, the Minister of Agriculture. The Minister of Agriculture in Nigeria is equivalent to the Secretary of Agriculture in the United States.

Shuaib's closeness to the president made him one of the formidable forces to reckon with at the Federal Executive Council in particular—the Armed Forces Ruling Council, as it was referred to at the time—and the entire nation in general. Aminu recollected how Umar had complained bitterly about Halima.

Umar never minced words, referring to Halima as the worst of all the spoiled brats he had seen. Halima, according to Umar, was not only unreasonable but extremely selfish, annoyingly possessive and with a serious anger-management issue. "She's not like Titi. She's not even anywhere close to Titi," Aminu recalled one of Umar's regular comments.

Their first two dates could be best described as dates in hell. Halima went nuts for the most inconsequential reasons, ranging from an untimely chair pull for her to the quality of the restaurant they had gone to. Despite being one of the best high-end restaurants in town, Halima referred to the place as being too cheap for her. She also accused Umar of being ten seconds late in pulling the chair out for her.

Aminu said he later advised Umar on the need to schedule a meeting with their dad to discuss Halima's disgusting attitude and why they were not a good fit. Unfortunately, their dad wouldn't listen to him. He wouldn't even have him say anything unpleasant about Halima. It looked more like the only thing that qualified Halima as a prospective daughter-in-law was her tribe.

The other factor was that Aliu hoped to utilize a relationship between Umar and Halima to further his relationship with Alhaji Abubakar Shuaib. He knew exactly what that meant for his business empire. With the superpower status of Shuaib, an upgrade from being a close friend to being an in-law would literally translate to more federal government contracts, more money, more power and greater influence. In all honesty, Aliu would have passed on the "more money, more power, and greater influence" opportunities if Titi was a Hausa girl.

Umar and Aminu knew that for a fact. So the only inference they could draw from their dad's preferential treatment of Halima was the fact that being a Hausa girl was all she needed to have an advantage over Titi. The focus was on her tribe. Not on her personality—and definitely not on Umar's happiness.

"Pressures from dad were humongous," Aminu added. Over and over again, their father convinced Umar that Halima would change for the better after marriage. Umar was finally coerced into a relationship with Halima and eventually into a marriage. Umar developed cold feet even before the wedding plans got underway, but his father acted more like a superman with a boast of repeated reassurances that he had everything under control.

Unfortunately, Halima graduated from an irritating and disgusting attitude to a thorn in the flesh. Umar was never happy—not even for a day. Halima was in the driver's seat of Umar's life. She called all the shots, even if the shots were not suitable for production. She wanted an explanation for every call on the home phone call log. She wanted an explanation if Umar returned home from work a minute past a certain time. She wanted to know everything that transpired between Umar and everyone else from the moment he left home in the morning and the time he returned home. Being home was hell for Umar. Halima choked him emotionally and tortured him psychologically.

Aminu recounted how Umar scheduled a meeting with him less than a week into the marriage. You could tell without being told that Umar had lost it. Everything he said to Aminu sounded more like he had a premonition of his own death. He said he knew the marriage would not, in any way, stand the test of time and wished his life would not end prematurely before the marriage ended abruptly.

His greatest concerns were Halima's anger-management issue, unreasonable attitude, illogical reasoning, constant defiant mood, extreme possessiveness, weird selfishness, bossy demeanor and being a habitual nag, among others. Aminu also shared with Titi how they both remembered how right their maternal uncle was. Uncle Citrus, as they fondly called him, once told them when they were both teenagers that a man should "avoid marrying a nagging woman and purchasing an old car if he wants to live long."

Unfortunately, Umar got entangled, not only in the web of a nagging wife but in the jaw and claws of the meanest of them all. His marriage to Halima only lasted for five months, but his life ended before the marriage did.

"How?!" Titi asked impatiently.

Aminu understood Titi's curiosity. He calmed down a little just to ensure Titi's nerves relaxed enough to prepare her mind for the final tragic event that snuffed the life out of the only man she ever cherished and loved just like a breeze would extinguish a lit candle.

Talking or thinking about that horrible story was always emotional for Aminu. No matter how hard he tried, it always got overwhelmingly emotional for him. He shut his eyes in a severe mental anguish, let out the tears, and then pulled himself together as he eventually satisfied Titi's curiosity.

"Halima stabbed him to death in a gruesome manner that has been described numerous times as the most heinous and most senseless murder ever."

It was over a trivial argument emanating from arriving home late from work. Umar explained to her that he had to work late to meet a deadline on a project he was working on—a story that was later corroborated by Umar's boss and colleagues after his death. Unfortunately, her history of impatience, anger issues and erratic behavior took over. She unjustly accused Umar of cheating on her. Then there was an argument. Then she became furious that Umar had the guts to argue with her. Then she reached for a boning knife. Then the devil incarnate wiped out Umar in an unimaginable callous manner with a total of twelve stabs.

Her anger fizzled as soon as she realized what she had done. She called my dad and stupidly reported herself as she cried her huge bulging eyes out of their shallow sockets. My dad called for help as he literally raced to their residence. Unfortunately, it was too late. Umar's body was labelled dead on arrival (DOA) as the medical team obviously couldn't do anything. I've never seen dad cry so profusely—in fact, I've never seen him cry at all. He cried uncontrollably, like a baby. In the days that followed Umar's death, he blamed himself for everything that happened and wished he had allowed Umar go with his choice—the Yoruba girl.

The entire family suffered mental turmoil after Umar's death. Not only did they lose Umar, but Alhaji Shuaib, Halima's dad, used his influence to prevent justice from being served. He did all he could within his political might and power to thwart justice. It took a combination of civil rights activists and a relentless brilliant legal team to bring Halima to trial.

There was an intermittent sob from Titi as Aminu narrated the pathetic story. Each time she sobbed, Aminu asked if she was okay. "I'll be fine," Titi would assure and reassure him. At the other end, Aminu would hesitate a little bit. Once Titi cleared her throat and wiped off the tears, she would simply say, "Please, continue," and Aminu would pick up from where he stopped.

Incredibly, the case dragged on forever before Halima was eventually found guilty and sentenced to life in prison without the possibility of parole. Aminu completed the sad story with the additional information that Alhaji Shuaib and his dad no longer saw eye to eye as the tragic event left a dent on their friendship.

The story was as tragic as much as pathetic. Titi struggled to find her next statement, as her mind was spinning. Her entire being blew up into several pieces. She exerted efforts to come up with a statement, but couldn't. Over the years, she had, obviously, been disturbed by Umar's mysterious disappearance, but she was not prepared for the tragic story that resolved the age-long mystery. For her, Umar's tragic death was one piece of bad news too many.

As she engaged her mind on coming up with the next thing to say to Aminu, her doorbell rang. The sound from the doorbell was loud enough for Aminu to hear at the other end.

"Sounds like you have a guest," Aminu said.

"Yes, that should be Lara—a friend that I'm expecting," Titi responded.

"What would be the most appropriate time to call you tomorrow?"

"Anytime that works for you is okay by me," Aminu reiterated.

"Okay, I'll call you sometime before bedtime," Titi promised as they bade each other goodnight.

Titi went straight for the door to let Lara in. Both of them had come a long way. She knew Titi's story and had always provided a shoulder to lean on. With no holds barred, Titi brought Lara up to speed on her latest discovery of the reason behind Umar's bizarre disappearance, from the dramatic connection with Aminu, Umar's brother, to the events that led to Umar's death.

It was a mixed discovery for Lara. She was devastated by Umar's tragic end on one hand, and relieved that Titi could now have closure on the other. She consoled Titi and also advised that she share her story with Aminu at their next meeting. "Someone needed to rub the story on Umar's dad's face just so he realizes the depth of the pain he inflicted on two love-birds as a result of his tribal sentiments," Lara furiously proposed.

CHAPTER 19:

RAYS OF LIGHT

There is no exercise better for the heart than reaching down and lifting people up.

– John Holmes

The next day, Titi called Aminu just before bedtime, as earlier agreed. She explained how she couldn't say a word the previous day due to the state of shock she was in. Aminu understood and advised her to get over the tragic news in the best way she could.

"So, what's been going on with you?" Aminu asked, trying to change the topic.

"It's been tough—so very tough," Titi admitted.

"Is it something you're willing to share?" Aminu asked.

"Sure." Titi responded. She then adjusted her recliner as she began to fill Aminu in on all that transpired after losing contact with Umar.

"Remember I told you the last time that I have been living a devastating life from the day your dad rejected me based on my tribe? Since then, I've always felt life has been unfair to me. My story is a little similar to that of Umar. The only difference is that Umar is dead and I'm dead alive. Just like your dad, my parents match-made me with a guy who was a son of a family friend. After several bouts of frustration, I agreed to give him a try against my wishes—after all, Umar was not forthcoming after I waited and searched for him for several years. Bayo Bucknor wasn't anything like Umar. Not even close. My parents turned deaf ears to my complaints about Bayo. Their conclusion was weird. They said a Yoruba guy is way better than a Hausa boy. Then, I was forced into a marriage that failed before it started.

"Bayo," Titi continued, "was successful in his career, a celebrated financial advisor who knew his professional strategies well. Everything he touched turned to gold. In no time, he became the Chief Operating Officer of the financial firm he worked for. He broke barriers, shattered glass ceilings and set new records. He successfully brokered deals in billions and eventually went on to set up his own financial firm."

"When he left the firm," Titi went on, "a handful of his colleagues dumped the firm in support of Bayo's dream. As soon as they pitched their tents with Bayo in what was described by business journals as an unprecedented new-generation innovation in the nation's business world, the Bizlink Group soon became a formidable force to reckon with—it was a one-stop financial firm that ventured into everything in the finance world. With just one year of operations, they shook the industry with unbelievable mergers and acquisitions that qua-drupled their market share and soon began to set up dedicated firms for specific markets.

"Within three years, Bizlink Advisors, Bizlink Investment, Bizlink Research and Development, Bizlink Capital and Bizlink Associates were all floated as affiliates of the parent company, Bizlink Group. Bayo had the vision, the concepts and with a durable and a sustainable strategy for his entire team, the dream and the concepts were actualized. Expectedly, the money trickled in. His former bosses became his strategic partners. They all scrambled for the crumps of Bizlink's major deals.

"However, Bayo's success had a limitation. His success started and ended in the business world. He failed very woefully in every other sphere of life. He was an embarrassment at home. His anger had no boundary. He talked down to everyone. He never apologized to anyone. He had a super-ego. He thought about himself alone. He was a chauvinist and an alcoholic. He blamed everyone around him. He did not take responsibility for any unpleasant outcome of his high-handedness. Above all, he was a career cheat and an unrepentant chain womanizer. As his business expanded, so was the enormity of the domestic abuse I contended with on the home front. "He treated me more like an invaluable possession. He came home whenever he liked. The result of an attempt by me to question his behavior always ended in chaos. His attitude was always that of 'how dare you ask me why I've not been home for days?' As if those hideous and repulsive characteristics of his were not enough, I became a steady punching bag readily available to receive physical and emotional blows. That was the deal-breaker for me. Although I saw the red lights before going into the marriage, I was blind-sided by my parents. They vouched for him endlessly. But he was a pretender. To my parents, two factors qualified him as a potential suitor: his tribe, as a Yoruba guy; and being a son of a family friend.

"With several visits that sometimes lasted for days at the local hospital after being brutally beaten, some folks still blamed me for having the guts to challenge Bayo for bringing his mistresses home. It was a rude awakening for me to realize how women's feelings are often treated as almost non-existent.

"I was literally expected to be mute when my supposed husband not only engaged in illicit and immoral extra-marital affairs outside of the home, but brought home his mistresses. I have blood that flows in my veins—I have feelings—I'm human—I'm a woman. I'm susceptible to emotional and mental torture. I'd heard and read about men who perceive women as creatures with gender inferiority, but it was a different ballgame when I experienced it first-hand. It's a crazy society we live in, a society that is vehemently cruel to women. A society where women receive not just a larger chunk of the blame, but all the blame.

"When a husband succeeds, he is a genius. When a husband fails, the failure is from the wife. When a man dies, his wife must have killed him. When a man choses to be irresponsible, the wife must have been responsible. When the kids are truants, their mother is the cause. When a man beats his wife, the wife gets blamed. When a man cheats on his wife, it's the fault of the woman. A heartless man receives an undeserved exoneration for his inhumane acts and shabby treatment of his wife, and the wife is treated as the aggressor.

"Of course, in every society, there are women aggressors, but the numerical strength of women in this category is too insignificant to warrant the unjustifiable stereotype. The bar seems to be too high for a woman. Annoyingly, the bar appears to get raised higher and higher from generation to generation.

"As Bayo's wife, I never had a good day. I cried when I woke up. I cried in the middle of the day. I cried all through the night. The old nursery rhyme of "Old McDonough had a farm" applied suitably to my situation. For me, instead of the everywhere moo-moo sound of cows, oink-oink sound of pigs, quack-quack sound of ducks and squeak-squeak sound of mice, it was cry-cry here, cry-cry there, everywhere cry-cry for me.

"One particular experience was the straw that broke the camel's back. As usual, Bayo brought home one of his mistresses supposedly for the weekend. I had seen several instances of his infidelity—countless times. But brandishing the infidelity in my face was the height of it. He beat me into a stupor when I told him how uncivilized his shameful daredevil adulterous acts were.

"My parents almost couldn't recognize me when they visited me at the hospital. My mom wept uncontrollably, seeing what I had to go through on a daily basis. It was the first time my parents openly blamed each other and admitted to have inadvertently misled me. They were even more shocked that he never even showed up at the hospital. How worthless can a man make his wife feel? When I eventually got okay, I went with my mind to save my life—divorce."

Aminu was astonished at the other end of the telephone. All he could say in between the graphic details of Titi's experience was an occasional "wow" that he let out incessantly as Titi wallowed in her pathetic lamentations. He remembered his brother and wondered why and how tribal differences could be allowed to prevail over love. Ironically, with all that Titi went through while she was married to Bayo, one would think she would stereotype men. Amazingly, she still strongly felt that life would have been a lot better with Umar. If only they had an opportunity to be together. Her life almost ended with Bayo and she blamed her parents for her near-death experience.

Somehow, at the drop of a hat, Aminu and Titi became the best of friends, united by the unpleasant events. Every now and then, they would call each other, compare notes on how their days went, share jokes, laugh and bid each other goodnight. The calls became a tradition. During one of those calls, they had both discussed Aminu extensively.

He shared with Titi how he vowed to himself never to get married with what befell his brother in the hands of Halima. It was the first time Titi realized Aminu was still single. She wondered why it never crossed her mind to ask after his wife or family in those late-night calls.

As days rolled into months, Aminu began to consider a possibility he personally considered crazy—the possibility of starting a relationship with Titi.

"Why not?" he would ask himself over and over again. "She's, no doubt, a virtuous woman who became a victim of tribalism. She deserves to be happy."

For some reason, the tradition of regular calls went from every other day to nightly. They soon became emotional about the nightly calls. Aminu certainly reminded Titi of Umar, and Titi somehow reminded Aminu of Umar as well.

Aminu made sure he asked Titi a couple of questions that cleared the air concerning whether she still carried a torch for her ex-husband. Needless to say, when it rains, it pours. It sounds like they were both eye to eye on the matter arising. So they began to make plans to physically meet with each other. The meeting kicked-off a passion that both sets of parents eventually got wind of. Unlike Umar and Titi, Aminu and Titi received tremendous support from both sides of the aisle.

Aminu's dad was all in, and Titi's parents had no choice. They supported Titi all the way. They were careful this time not to make happiness elusive for their daughter. Both parents seemed to have found an efficacious therapy for their tribal ailments.

In the days that preceded their marriage, Aminu's dad had never seen him that happy. Kunle and Biola, on their part, remembered vividly well that the last time they saw their daughter that happy was before they threw a clog in the wheel of her relationship with Umar.

This time, they made sure they saw Aminu as human and not as a Hausa boy.

Several facts were revealed when Titi and Aminu started their relationship. One of them was the similarity between Aminu and Umar in term of respect, care and unprecedented passion they brought into their relationships, of which Titi was a beneficiary. Aminu, for his part, realized why his brother was always extremely happy and fulfilled while he was in the relationship with Titi. She had a lot to offer: friendship, affection and dependability.

Aliu became happy again for the first time after the tragic loss of Umar. He needed no one to tell him that an objection was not an option. It would be devastating to risk losing another child. With Aminu's obvious happiness, tribalism, by extension, was one thing that he learned to nip in the bud the hard way.

So, he got the drift this time. In no time, Aliu became friends with Kunle and Biola. He then realized how distinguished they both are and vice versa—a case of once bitten, twice shy. This time, both parents ensured that Aminu and Titi did not go cold turkey on their marriage plans: They received all the support they could ever ask for. It was a tremendous support as both parents and families wrapped their arms around them.

How time flies. The wedding day was here before they knew it. The scheduled date was heralded by a culture confluence, the Yoruba autochthonous tradition manifested through customs and arts and the Hausa rich folk culture exhibited through folk songs and traditional aerobic dance steps. The city of Lagos seldom witnessed such a superlative grandeur of classy cross-cultural display in one single event. On the bandstand were two prominent bands representing the two tribes, the Arewa Band of Hausa extraction from the north and the Silver Highlife Band of Yoruba extraction from the south. At some point, both bands performed simultaneously in a melodic blend of sonorous voices and percussions that produced harmonious rhythms and danceable beats that left guests yearning and clamoring for more.

Historically, Yoruba and Hausa weddings are always beautiful sights to behold. With a combination of both cultures in one event, it was a case of two irresistible products for the price of one—buy one, get one free (BOGOF). Though Aminu and Titi wore matching attire, Titi's was with a Yoruba touch while Aminu's was with a Hausa blend. Their attire was a combination of royal blue and snow white hand-knitted fabric popularly referred to as *aso oke*.

The bride was usually the day's center of attraction. Her *aso oke* was a blouse with simple but elegant embroidery with a flowing wrapper called *iro*. The *iro* was stylishly tied around her waist and flowed through her hips all the way to her feet. The lower edge touched on the floor with every step made. She had on a spiral scarf—headgear locally referred to as *gele*. The *gele* had a slight color contrast with the blouse, but matched the *iro* very perfectly. Guests, friends and family members were not disappointed as everything the bride had on was an expression of style, class and elegance.

On a good day, outside of an occasion like this, Aminu was a trendy kind of guy. Just like his late brother Umar, his fashion taste was incredibly immense. They got it from dad. He had on a white traditional shirt and pants referred to as *babariga* with a flowing royal blue regalia called *agbada* on top of the *babariga*. The embroidery in front of the *agbada* mimicked a royal symbol of a monarchical dynasty. His hat had the same embroidery, but in a smaller version of the design. His striped dress shoe was customized for the occasion; it was a laminate of the *aso oke* material. The shoes served their purpose as they were meant to match his *agbada*.

Those who knew about the strong racist views of Aliu and his prejudice against folks outside of his tribe initially took it with a grain of salt when they heard over the grapevine that his would-be in-laws were Yoruba people. Essentially, the situation put them between a rock and a hard place until the wedding got underway. Against all initial odds for the Olofin and the Rafiu families, Aminu and Titi tied the knot amid funfair to the admiration of all and sundry. Interestingly, both parents became strong advocates of anti-racism/anti-tribalism crusades afterwards, and Titi and Aminu have both lived happily ever after.

CHAPTER 20:
THE CORONA EFFECT

Too often we underestimate the power of a touch, a smile,
a kind word, a listening ear, an honest compliment, or the
smallest act of caring, all of which have the potential to
turn a life around.

– Leo F. Buscaglia

Decades after the tragic story of Titi and Umar turned into the heartwarming story of Titi and Aminu, a never-before-seen pandemic hit the world. Historically, the world has had its share of plagues and epidemics. These epidemics have ravaged humanity across all centuries with different categories of severity. Some of them include:

I.   Plague of Athens (430 BC)

II.   Antonine Plague (AD 165–180)

III.   Plague of Cyprian (AD 250–271)

IV.   Plague of Justinian (AD 541–542)

V.   The Black Death (1346–1353)

VI.   Cocoliztli epidemic (1545–1548)

VII.   American Plagues (16th century)

VIII. Great Plague of London (1665–1666)

IX.   Great Plague of Marseille (1720–1723)

X.   Russian Plague (1770–1772)

XI.   Philadelphia Yellow Fever Epidemic (1793)

XII.   Flu Pandemic (1889–1890)

XIII. American Polio Epidemic (1916)

XIV.   Spanish Flu (1918–1920)

XV.   Asian Flu (1957–1958)

XVI.   AIDS Pandemic and Epidemic (1981–present)

XVII. H1N1 Swine Flu Pandemic (2009–2010)

XVIII. Ebola Epidemic (2014–2016)

XIX.   Zika Virus Epidemic (2015–present)

However, when Covid-19 began between the last quarter of 2019 and the first quarter of 2020, it showed up with compelling intimidation. With its highly contagious status and ability to shatter the human artery and halt the respiratory system, Covid-19 instantaneously became a game changer—the commander-in-chief of all epidemics.

It began from the city of Wuhan, the capital of Hubei Province in central China, and hit the entire world like a wildfire powered by an uncontrollable turbulent wind. As soon as it hit, it swiftly traversed the world, and the entire world with everything in it stood still.

Once an infected droplet is inhaled, the virus finds its way into the human body, invades the cells and begins to replicate itself. During the process of replication, it attacks new cells and eventually hits the lungs. At that point, life begins to tick towards a zero hour.

Testing positive for Covid-19 was more like a death sentence. The number of deaths was not only unprecedented, it was astronomic. The numerical strength of healthcare workers was no match for the influx of patients to the hospitals. They just couldn't handle the volume, not even with the number of makeshift hospitals that sprang up everywhere. Funnily enough, the so-called superpower nations scrambled for solutions unsuccessfully as citizens were lost to the epidemic in the millions.

The global economy came under threat. The stock market witnessed the worst market volatility ever. Trade activities went just one way—south. It eventually exceeded the set thresholds hitting the circuit-breaker points and halting trade activities market-wide. The global economy was hit in no time. Employees were either laid off or furloughed in the face of what was perceived as an imminent recession.

Small businesses closed down indefinitely, forcing their workers to become economic orphans in addition to being socially disconnected. The unemployment rate surged to a two-digit number overnight, while applications for unemployment benefits reached a record high. Mega-cities across the globe literally became ghost towns as government after government gave shelter-in-place orders. Then, the streets became desolate afterwards. It was a humongous disaster— the type the world has never witnessed—a global house arrest of all humans. Researchers and scientists scrambled for medical solutions to deflate the pandemic's mass-destroyer ego. Husbands were separated from their wives and parents kept a safe distance from their kids.

Mainstream media reporters and broadcasters reported and broadcast from home. The entire world did not only stand still, it turned around and began to move backwards. Unfortunately, every strategy adopted by world leaders failed as the issue defied solutions. Indeed, it was an era characterized by an abnormal new normal.

As the death toll continued to rise in the face of global economic uncertainty, the conventional trajectory changed just as the status quo became modified. All of a sudden, the crime rate dropped dramatically. Specifically, the rate of sporadic mass shootings dropped considerably. Humans began to show love to one another more than ever before even in the face of social distancing and shelter-in-place orders. Billionaires and successful corporate entities began to donate money in billions to assist in the areas of Covid-19-inclined research and support for victims.

In addition, governments across the globe began to mitigate the gravity of the devastating effects of the pandemic through stimulus packages for their citizens. Ironically, the world did not see any of the superpower nations roll out artilleries, guns, ammunition, or missiles to combat Covid-19, despite the acquisition of enormous economic and military power.

Yet, with no single shot fired by the virus, it crept into different nations, and made its way through heavily fortified borders—past the military, immigration authorities, and customs into the streets, workplaces, public places, healthcare facilities, and homes, wreaking a never-before-seen havoc. The police couldn't get it arrested with all the super-advanced technology in the intelligence arena. Then the virus killed millions without a single shot fired.

Wait a minute! Is God trying to tell us something? Are nations making the wrong investments? Is there a destructive enemy that could possibly invade a powerful nation undetected? Would there ever be a time when an enemy will penetrate the borders with a motive to kill and yet a powerful military wouldn't be able to fight back?

Is there anything that will suddenly pose a threat to a set of people who consider themselves as being super healthy? Would there ever be an insurgent who bears no arms and yet would kill with no discrimination?

The focus here is not on the cause of the pandemic or the degree of responsiveness of governments around the globe to human safety and protection. Neither is the focus on evaluating emerging facts, conflicting stories and conspiracy theories behind the outbreak of the deadly pandemic. Rather, the focus here is on what is derivable from the unpleasant situation that might have the ability of advancing the course of humanity.

With the dastardly act of the virus, the answers are not far-fetched. Covid-19 did not look at the color of the skin before striking. Neither did it take nationality or social class into consideration before infecting people. This monster is a leveler who spends the night in a palatial mansion of an exclusive and extremely wealthy neighborhood and wakes up in the morning in a grimy dilapidated residence of a tattered neighborhood. It just doesn't care who its victims are. It has one and only one target—humans.

Are there lessons to learn from the pandemic? What exactly is the cost of love? What exactly do people lose by loving people across the board? Why should the world wait for a disaster of the magnitude perpetuated by Covid-19 for humans to unite?

A sovereign nation has the right to fortify its military in an attempt to protect its citizens and territorial integrity, but it shouldn't look away from the divisive rancor that tears those citizens apart internally. Humanitarian initiatives equally deserve a considerable amount of investment.

Governance is all about humanity. From foreign diplomacy to the administration of justice. From provision of public services to the protection of civil liberties, humans are right at the center of governance. A Department of Humanitarian Affairs would go a long way if established and saddled with the responsibility of collaborating with existing departments to champion the course of humanity. The Department of Humanitarian Affairs, in the spirit of championing the course of humanity, needs to ensure that the Department of Health puts in place every mechanism needed to detect and forestall possible outbreaks of pandemics in the future.

The department should also collaborate with other departments to ensure humans are cared for across the board. It should also launch laudable programs as well as crusades for peaceful coexistence. If a one-digit percentage of what is spent on weapon acquisition instead went into a dedicated initiative that preaches love and unity, then Yay!—a more peaceful world is a certainty. In the face of a virus-ravaged world, there is need for love to be the pivot upon which our everyday living swings. Love and tolerance of one another across the line of race and ethnicity are golden.

CHAPTER 21;
A PATH TO PEACE

It is easy enough to be friendly to one's friends. But to befriend the one who regards himself as your enemy is the quintessence of true religion. The other is mere business.

– Mahatma Gandhi

It is very glaring that the scourge of racism and tribalism has ravaged our world. Humans naturally advocate for their races—not necessarily for humanity. A closer look at our world reveals that humans have not only figured out a way to unravel mysteries surrounding how organisms relate to one another in the system of ecology, they have also cleverly mastered how to live in peace with different creatures.

Marine biologists dive into deep blue seas to closely study aquatic animals. Mammalogy experts and adventure-seekers visit the Amazon and Serengeti to cohabit with animals and study their lifestyles. Some animal lovers have successfully domesticated wild animals.

Historically, humans have literally changed the way humans live over the centuries. Innovative minds have transformed and completely revolutionized the world we live in through divergent life-changing inventions, which include but are not limited to the list I selected for this table.

Car	Lens	Car tires
Incandescent light bulb	Aircraft	Submarine
Television	Internal combustion engine	Electric generator
Camera	Film	Cotton gin
Internet	Printing press	Cathode
Telephone	Bicycle	Transistor
Electric battery	Penicillin	Radar
Steam engine	Photography	Glasses
Telescope	Mobile phone	Video
Lens	Radio	Electric motor
Aircraft	Paper	Word Wide Web
Microscope	Calculator	ARPANET
Turbine	Screw	Assembly line
Compass	Morse code	Jet engine
Phonograph	Optical fiber	Diesel engine
Pump	Gunpowder	Cathode-ray tube
Alternating current	Vacuum tube	Electrical telegraph

These inventions are life-changing, but the most impactful inventions are in the areas of science and technology. Interestingly, they have touched on aviation, telecommunication, transportation, outer space, security and human interaction—literally everything. Without a doubt, Alexander Graham Bell wouldn't recognize what the telephone, his pet invention, has turned into in the twenty-first century. One can only imagine what life and living would have been like without these inventions. The elastic nature of human imagination and creativity is astronomical.

Regrettably, with all the laudable achievements in the areas of life-changing inventions and unbelievable ability to study and live with animals, humans have not succeeded in living with one another peacefully. There are imaginary partitions and stratifications along the lines of race, tribe and ethnicity. There is no unifying factor with humans as common denominators.

I'm not an expert on religion, but with an Advanced Diploma in Theology, I know enough to posit that most religions understand the principle of love and lay emphasis on it as an antidote to hate as a result of its proven propensity to enhance and promote peace. For instance, in the Holy Bible, the gospel according to Saint Mathew, Chapter 22, focuses on topics that could be split into five different categories:

- The parable of the Wedding Banquet.
- Paying the Imperial Tax to Caesar.
- Marriage at the Resurrection.
- The Greatest Commandment.
- Whose Son is the Messiah?

Under 'The Greatest Commandment" segment, Verses 37 to 39 highlight the importance of the love of God and instruct that we love our neighbors as ourselves. This instruction was in response to a Pharisee who was a law expert. This law expert had requested from Jesus to know what the greatest commandment in the law was. These verses have been evaluated by Bible scholars at different periods of time and they've all concluded that the "love thy neighbor" commandment has a connotative meaning, as the word "neighbor" was used figuratively.

In other words, if implying other than an explicit expression of "neighbor" is anything to go by, then "neighbor," as portrayed in

Verse 39, does not necessarily translate to next-door folks exclusively. Rather, it implies family members, friends, co-workers, total strangers—in fact, everyone. All humans across the board. All humans—race, tribe, social class and political affiliations notwithstanding. Love is everything. It covers a multitude of sins.

According to First Peter, Chapter 4, Verse 8, "Above all, love one another deeply, because love covers over a multitude of sins." Here, Peter, an apostle of Jesus, in his first epistle to the strangers scattered throughout Pontus, Galatia, Cappadocia, Asia and Bithynia, instructs everyone to love everyone, because love, in itself, covers a multitude of sins.

I've been a part of discussion groups where this instruction from Peter's epistle was evaluated and unfortunately misinterpreted. Some folks have an erroneous notion that once you love, in obedience to this instruction, it's probably a license to commit other sins as you are "covered" by the fact that you love everyone.

However, the truth is that what "love covers over a multitude of sins" means is that the ability of humans to love all humans prevents humans from committing other sins. For instance, when you love everyone without prejudice—within and outside of your race, tribe and ethnicity—the world will, no doubt, be a better place to live in.

In other words, when an individual loves people generally across the board, that individual is not going to steal from people, kill people, hurt people, rape people, lie against people, seek for people's downfall and discriminate against people based on their races or tribes. So with unconditional love, one can only imagine the list of menaces that would be eliminated from society.

The instruction to love everyone by Apostle Peter is an offshoot of an earlier evaluation of love by Solomon, the son of King David, in Proverbs, Chapter 10, Verse 12: "Hatred stirs up conflict, but love covers over all wrongs" (New International Version, NIV). Here, Solomon, the wisest human who ever lived, successfully evaluated hatred and love as well as their aftermaths in the same verse.

The result of his evaluation is a pointer to the fact that racism and tribalism do not precede hatred, but hatred precedes them all. If Solomon's evaluation is anything to go by, racism, tribalism, ethnicity, chaos, war, bitterness and animosity are some of the conflicts stirred by hatred, just as love and kindness precede peace.

I'm a first-generation immigrant to the United States. I've been at different fora where fellow immigrants take turns sharing their experiences when they first relocated to the United States. I've heard stories that ranged from surviving hostile hosts to culture shock, but each time they compare their notes with mine, everyone always feels extremely fortunate as their experiences are those of luxury compared to mine.

I started with homelessness from day one. I prayed and wished for a hostile host. I flew in to JFK (John F. Kennedy Airport, New York). There I was in the land of the free and the home of the brave, but with no family members or friends. An old friend of mine had refused to pick my calls in the days preceding my relocation to the United States—this was after I requested the favor of hosting me.

I had a very good job and a thriving business on the side. I gave them all up for the proverbial American dream. There I was on a U.S.-bound airplane with absolutely no idea where I was going to put up. As soon as the airplane touched ground, every passenger disembarked.

I did as well, went through immigration checks, and headed straight to the baggage claim area where I grabbed my belongings and headed for the streets afterwards.

I watched as car after car pulled up at the arrivals pickup area to pick their loved ones, but none came for me. I was all alone in a strange land clad in a shirt and dress pants in one-digit weather. With a wind gust way above average, the weather felt more like below zero.

In less than five minutes, I started to shiver like a malfunctioning engine that just lost a vital part responsible for its running smoothly. My lower and upper lips began to slam against each other involuntarily, producing a weird sound that was out of rhythm. For the first time in my life, all my limbs went numb on me. My carry-on bag fell off my shoulder, and as I bent over to pick it up, I discovered that I couldn't keep a firm grip on the bag as I struggled to get it off the snow-covered ground.

Expectedly, my fingers lost their grip and the other luggage slipped slightly to the side of the road. At this time, my hands were completely frozen, and then I began to have a strange feeling internally. It felt more like all my internal organs had filed out on a single queue, sending signals to my brain that they were right on the verge of shutting down one after the other.

What could be best described as a shortness of breath followed the sinister signals in a quick succession. At this point, I knew I had to look for some kind of warmth in the next minute; otherwise I might possibly become unconscious, wake up on the other side, and begin to hang out with my ancestors.

In a split second, as the thought of a possible fraternity with my ancestors flashed through my mind, I left my luggage by the side of the road and sprinted back into the airport with a speed that would place Usain Bolt in a distant second place behind me if he had been in that race with me.

Once inside, I literally dropped on one of the benches from across the concession area designated for the airlines. I gasped and gasped for breath as New Yorkers walked past me without noticing my near-death experience—a first dose of welcome to New York!

I could tell that my body temperature had drastically dropped. About three minutes of warmth made all the difference. All my internal organs began to disembark from their initial positions on the single-file queue and I heaved a euphoric sigh of relief as they went back to their normal positions and resumed their different regular functions. I then rushed back outside, retrieved my luggage, and came back in to savor more warmth.

By the time I recovered fully, I realized how close I had been to hypothermia. Incredibly, with nowhere to go in a strange land, JFK Airport became my first apartment, the bench became my first bed and my carry-on luggage—my first pillow.

The next day, I called my family members—my parents and siblings. I told them I had a safe trip but I didn't tell them I was homeless. By nature, I'm very independent and detest anything that will amount to, look like, or sound like a search for sympathy. The third day, I was not only feeling uncomfortable in the same shirt and pants, I also felt I needed to change strategy. I'd been moving around within the airport, as well as switching sleep areas to avoid being noticed as a stranded traveler by the airport security officials and risking being sent to the streets.

At about four p.m. on my third day of homelessness, I decided to check into a hotel. The issues with this decision started to trickle into my mind. What happens when you run out of money? Where would you go? How would you eat? With those questions, I knew there was need for me to conserve the money I had left on me.

First and foremost, I needed to leave the airport before I become a subject of suspicion. It was in the middle of a decision-making process that I remembered an old pen-pal. Folks of my generation will remember what pen-pals were all about, especially in the high school days.

Pen-pals were like social groups back in the day. For the most part, you would find them either in groups or as individuals in foreign magazines, pick one who catches your interest, copy his or her address and begin an endless exchange of correspondence.

One of my regular pen-pals was Mykel Board. We used to exchange letters when I was in high school. As technology evolved at the time, we graduated to exchanging e-mails. He was the founder of The World for Free, a social group of travelers. As a matter of fact, it was one of the original social networks. The idea behind the formation of the group was to foster a good relationship among members worldwide.

Once a good friendship is established, you can inform such member whenever you are traveling to his or her side of the world, and if both parties have a mutual agreement, you can stay with such a member for free for the duration of your visit to that part of the world. The duration of stay depends on the agreement between both parties.

From the past letters that we exchanged, I remembered Mykel lived on Bleecker Street in the Manhattan Area of New York, and from visualizing one of his letters, I was able to recollect the house number. I decided to give the address a shot. So I put my stuff together, left my airport abode and walked to the taxi stand within the airport. I informed the first cab guy I spoke with of my destination address. He then helped put my luggage in the trunk, drove me to Bleecker Street and charged me 80 bucks, which I promptly paid. From my accent, he knew I was new in town. It took me a couple of cab and subway rides around the city a few weeks later to realize that the cab driver ripped me off—Welcome to New York!

Though I informed Mykel of my U.S. trip while I was doing the paperwork, I never planned to barge in on him. The decision to try him out was a risky one. I was very hesitant, but I had no choice. This was me planning to seek for a favor from someone I'd never seen physically. And to make matters worse, I was doing it without prior notice. How more inconsiderate could I be? Eventually, the house number turned out to be a high-rise apartment complex. It took me a few hours before I located Mykel. In those hours, I had to contend with the cold all over again. He was not home and I didn't know what floor he lived on. Occasionally, I went in and out of the corner stores and restaurants to keep myself warm.

I sat on my luggage at the main entrance of the apartment complex building, shivering from the cold. I was about making another trip to any other available open public place close by to keep myself warm, when Mykel eventually arrived. I recognized him from the earlier pictures we had exchanged. I walked up to him and introduced myself. He recognized me as soon as I mentioned my name. He also may have recognized my face as I stood in front of him narrating my ordeal of being stranded at the airport and not having anyone to pick me up.

Mykel surprised me with his act of kindness. He helped me with my luggage as he ushered me to the elevator and took me in—into his apartment. He knew how cold I was and made me a hot coffee.

He showed me the bathroom afterwards, where I had my first shower in four days. That night, I let out all the Zzsssss and slept like a baby. Mykel hosted me for a couple of weeks or so.

He took me out almost every other night to meet his friends. Sometimes, I would wake up to see notes addressed to me from Mykel beside the bed with detailed information of where he would be after work as well as directions of how to get there and join him for fun. I had to eventually pretend to him that I was leaving New York in search of an old friend, as I didn't want to be a burden to him; I guess my independent nature set in. Several years after, Mykel's selflessness and kindness to me still resonate with me. We are not of the same race and I'm somewhat of a total stranger, yet he took me in without prior notice and provided me with shelter and friendship when I needed them the most.

I checked into a hotel and spent the next couple of days trying to figure out what I needed to do. Eventually, I concluded that the land of the free and home of the brave was probably not meant for me. At the end of the day, I decided to dump the proverbial American dream and go back to my country, Nigeria. Although I would no longer have a job, it would be an opportunity to pick my business back up, devote a hundred percent of my time to it and build it to the height that I envisioned when I set it up. So I called Funke, my sister, and told her my ordeal for the first time and my decision to come back home. But then she didn't agree with any of my reasons to come back home. She reminded me of how I'd always been a warrior—a fighter and not a quitter. She encouraged me to hold on firmly to the wheel of progress and soldier on.

Afterwards, Funke spoke with Femi, her husband, who connected me with Gboyega, his old friend who lives in Atlanta. I called him and we had a good conversation. He then promised to host me if I decided to leave New York for Atlanta. I did just that when I was on the verge of running out of money for hotel bills. Once in Atlanta, I began to make frantic efforts all by myself in a new country and a new city.

CHAPTER 22:

KINDNESS—PASS IT ON

*It is an absolute human certainty that no one can know
his own beauty or perceive a sense of his own worth until
it has been reflected back to him in the mirror of another
loving, caring human being.*

– John Joseph Powell

Speaking about loving and caring human beings and how kindness could unite the human race, make the world go round, and
eradicate racism and tribalism—the bane of our existence—I met
extraordinary people and experienced exemplary acts of kindness.

Dr. Albert and Mary Salako

Following all the frantic efforts, I got a job with Corporate Ventures
Systems. It wasn't a skilled position. So I struggled to stay afloat at
the initial stage as I never had a blue-collar job. I believe anything
that is worth doing at all is worth doing well. With that in mind, I
swallowed my pride and performed duties assigned to me diligently.
Dr. Albert and Mary his wife owned the company at the time. Having
realized the fact that I was not only new in town, but also new in the
United States, they asked me to move into their house. That kind

gesture helped me a lot. Mary is an exceptionally nice lady. She treated me more like a family member. To show my appreciation, I always stepped in to manage the business whenever Dr. Albert travelled out of town—from general administration to preparing invoices for clients, and from processing workers' payroll to conducting interviews for prospective new workers.

With all the challenges of working night and day shifts seven days of the week, I enrolled full-time for a graduate degree. My daily routine was from work to school and from school to all-night work. For the most part, the days I had one hour of sleep were super lucky days for me. After the MBA class, I got a job offer with a financial firm whose global headquarters is in St. Louis, Missouri.

Mark and Cherie Ellis

Following my acceptance of the job offer, I moved to St Louis. It was on the job that I met Mark. His family became the first family I met in the St Louis area. Despite the fact that Mark was not part of the interview panel that conducted all the several stages of the interview for me, surprisingly, he showed a lot of interest in my welfare. The first team meeting that I attended, our boss introduced me to the rest of the team as "the new guy on the team who is not only new on the job, but also new in town."

Mark walked up to my desk after the meeting to personally introduce himself and offered to be of help if I ever needed assistance for anything. As I contemplated whether to take him up on that offer or not, Mark sent me an e-mail on Friday of the same week asking me to join him and his family over the weekend if I was ever bored all alone in my hotel room. Cherie, his wife, actually stopped by at the office that Friday. Mark asked me to come with him to the first floor, where I met Cherie and they both ended up giving me a ride to my hotel.

That weekend, I couldn't go to his house as the trucker expected to transport my car from Atlanta hadn't delivered it yet. Eventually, my car was delivered, so I made it to Mark's house the following weekend and met Darien, his son, who was also as cool and as nice as his parents. They extended hands of friendship to me. Within a short while, I became a part of their family. They never left me out in any of their family plans. I went on road trips with them to see Cherie's family in Ohio several times.

Mark is one guy who will willingly go out of his way to make everyone comfortable. He does not have the "me" mentality. He looks at situations and specifically searches for the opportunities in them for all.

Cherie is a very selfless lady. Super-selfless for the most part. She's exceptionally kind, with an impeccable character. She considers others before herself. She'll do anything to make people around her happy. In one of the numerous times they invited me over for dinner, Cherie surprised me with a Nigerian dish. She had done extensive research and retrieved recipes online just to make me feel at home. Cherie epitomizes kindness for real.

I was not in any way surprised to discover that Mark and Cherie both sponsor the education of a random needy kid in Peru. They also demonstrated a good spirit of friendship and expressed the depth of their trust for me when they left their son and home in my care during one of their trips out of the country. Their offer of friendship combated loneliness for me in a tremendous way. They provided me a reliable and a dependable shoulder to rest on when I needed one the most.

Yet, we are not of the same race. If the world is filled with the likes of Mark and Cherie, hate that breeds racism and tribalism will have no chance in our world and global peace will be assured.

Tom and Sharon Seibert

Tom and Sharon are the second couple I met in the St. Louis area. They are both two of a kind. They never paid attention to skin color. They see people across the board as humans. We just clicked and bonded from the moment I met them despite being of different races. They are the same age as my parents. They call me their son, and I call them my adopted parents. I've gone everywhere with them. They introduced me to all of their biological children, grandchildren and great grandchildren. Awesome is the most appropriate single word that describes them.

They offer me their hands of friendship anytime. Tom and Sharon will call me to check if it's okay for them to stop over at my place. They'll show up and share different interesting stories with me—how they met, what growing up was like for them, the issues they encountered as husband and wife, how they overcame those issues, the good times they've had together, their plans and so many more.

They'll tell me to always reach out to them if I ever need anything. I've been so blessed to learn from them. They are very rich in wisdom and it's an opportunity of a lifetime that our paths crossed. I love them so very dearly for so many reasons: They are selfless, ever willing to be there, always want to see you smile and much more.

Once a powerful storm hit the city where my parents live in Nigeria. By the time the storm settled, there was great devastation. The fence of my parents' house had collapsed and the roof was literally blown off. The entire community was in total chaos.

My parents narrowly escaped death. There was no warning, as the entire community is not historically prone to natural disaster let alone a disaster of that magnitude. My parents took refuge at their local church and I sent them money to commence repairs immediately. I saw

Tom and Sharon a couple of days after and shared the story with them. I then asked them to keep my parents in their thoughts and prayers.

Tom and Sharon did not only pray for my parents, they showed up at my place with a check for my parents to cover part of the repair cost. I turned it down, letting them know I already sent them money for the same purpose. Tom and Sharon insisted and I insisted as well. They left after spending time with me, and then called me later to let me know that they tucked the check inside my couch since I didn't want to collect it.

At that point, I saw the genuineness of their intention to be part of the repair efforts, so I cashed the check and sent it to my parents. I told them it was from Tom and Sharon. They appreciated it and sent Tom and Sharon their appreciation.

One day, Tom and Sharon invited me to a musical event. They were both active participants at the event, so they were right on the stage. As the event was underway, the guy who sat next to me decided to start a conversation with me. He introduced himself as Larry and I introduced myself as well. We were both enjoying the event when Larry suddenly tapped me on the shoulder and pointed in the direction of Tom and Sharon. He actually didn't realize that I knew them. "See that couple by the piano?" Larry asked, as I nodded my head in affirmation of the fact that I'd seen them and waiting patiently for what he had to say about them. "It's amazing the way they love people—they just love people," Larry informed me.

I shared the story with Tom and Sharon afterwards. That tells me more about them. What if all of us as humans were conscious of what the guy sitting next to the guy who knows us would say about us when we are not listening? We would be more careful about the way we conduct ourselves and most importantly, the way we relate with people within and outside of our race.

Steve and Jacquie Junker

Everyone should wish for a Steve and Jacquie as friends. Have you ever heard of a twelve-midnight friend? A friend who is willing to act as a friend any time of day? A friend you could call when he or she is asleep in the middle of the night and who would jump up to do anything for you? That's the kind of friends Steve and Jacquie are.

I met them through Tom and Sharon, and they have been more than wonderful. Our friendship is more like a bond. We share so many things in common. People around me could tell, from my advocacy for a peaceful world through kindness to one another to my crusade of unity for the entire human race, that I do not see skin color. I only see people as humans—skin color notwithstanding. Steve and Jacquie share the same ideology.

This couple took friendship to a whole new level when I had Doyin, my second son. Aside from being excited for me, Jacquie stood with us all through the process. It was a long labor for my wife and Jacquie spent two straight nights with us at the hospital. She was right there with us in the delivery room, providing all the support we needed.

They both did the same thing during the birth of my third son. I've never seen a couple with such wonderful hearts of gold. Family members are thousands of miles away from us, so Steve and Jacquie perfectly played the roles of family members to us. Steve is an easy-going perfect gentleman with a good sense of humor. Whenever he speaks, he speaks wisdom. Jacquie, on the other hand, mixes very freely with people. She possesses the uncommon gift of a superlative friendly disposition with a good spirit.

Both of them are excellent with kids. They are always super-excited whenever it is time to go visit their grandkids, Lumen and Ember in South Carolina. They talk about them with a great deal of passion. Amazingly, they extend the same amount of passion to kids who are not biologically linked to them.

In addition to the reliable and dependable friendship offered to us by this amazing couple, Jacquie babysat my second son for months for free. I literally implored her to accept cash payments for her services, but she turned down my offer over and over again despite my insistence. "He's like a grandson to me," she would say each time I brought up the idea of paying her.

The boys grew up to see her as a grandmother figure and address her as such. Yet we are not of the same race. Imagine a world with more Steves and Jacquies. Imagine the enormity of the global peace their likes would ensure.

Harold and Jami Woods

Harold and Jami both epitomize what could be best described as blindness to skin color. No matter what your race is, this couple sees people as humans. They do not believe, peddle, share or hold sentiments that are race-inclined.

I refer to Harold as "big brother" and he calls me "lil brother." I was alone all by myself when I moved to the St. Louis area—no wife, no kids. I was just a Lone Ranger of sorts. He was one of the folks who combated boredom that attempted to contend with me, especially after each day's work at the office and over the weekends.

Harold would not only invite me to join him and his friends for a ping-pong game, he also invited me to his house several times for dinner. Jami was always available to make me feel at home. She's such an amazing cook. She'll not let me leave until I had enough to eat, and having enough to eat won't stop her from putting together enough "to go" for me. "I know you don't cook much as a bachelor," she would say while getting the "to go" together.

Jami extended a hand of friendship to my wife when my bachelor's status changed. She'll come over to our house to keep her company when I'm gone to the office. At the time, my wife was relatively new in town. She would drive her around town and show her places of interest: the malls, the stores, the parks.

This couple's kindness never stopped. When my sister and her husband visited, Harold and Jami showed up to take them out. My sister and her husband couldn't stop talking about how nice Harold and Jami were to them. This couple are of the same race as me but we are of different nationalities. Imagine the depth of peace the world would have experienced if everyone lived with open arms of acceptance to everyone within and outside of their races like Harold and Jami.

Byron and Kyong Jimerson

This couple lives a life of service to humanity. Amazingly, beneficiaries of their act of service to humanity are not predefined by race. People in their lives cut across all races, as skin color does not stand in the way of who they relate to. Byron has a great friendly disposition, exhibits a great deal of humility and sees people generally as humans.

Kyong has a great personality and mixes freely with everyone. While everyone relaxes at home or visit fun spots at leisure times, Kyong spends her leisure time, for the most part, visiting assisted living and nursing homes as a volunteer caring for people who are either abandoned by their family members or too ill or old to engage in basic care for themselves. At other times, she just randomly offers companionship to lonely people who need it the most. She does this with no race preference.

Sometime, I had a work-related emergency that required me to be physically available in the office. With the shortest amount of notice—same day, in this situation—Kyong, in her magnanimity, accepted to watch my son who was less than a year old at the time. Her private business requires her to actively attend to clients all of the time. Amazingly, she partially shut down some of her daily operations to fully attend to my son. Yet we are not of the same race.

Byron and Kyong sure live an exemplary life. What they engage each other in, in the area of service to humanity, is the true definition of kindness that can make the world go round.

Dave and Dawnetta Hornyak

One can definitely beat one's chest and heave a heavy sigh of relief if one has an opportunity to have Dave and Dawnetta on one's contact list. Dave is more like a humor merchant. He does not apply the stress that comes with everyday living to life. He's one of the people I've seen who lives life with ease. He brings out humor in every situation.

Dawnetta, on the other hand, is the most kind-hearted person around. She gives the best hug in the entire world. Her hugs go beyond the traditional exchange of pleasantries; they are assurances of genuine care and expressions of unprecedented kindness.

She's that special someone who wants to see a smile on people's faces all the time. She's that special someone you would hope shows up when you are not having a good day. She carries hope, care and love with her everywhere she goes.

In my lonely days, Dave and Dawnetta invited me over to their house for lunch and dinner a couple of times. They are great hosts. From the stories they shared with me, I deduced that they met while in high school, and they still relate to each other lovingly like they just met the previous day.

When I had my sons Doyin and Dola, Dawnetta showed up at our door with delicious home-cooked meals as soon as my wife got home from the hospital. We couldn't ask for a more thoughtful friend; she knew my wife won't be strong enough to prepare meals for us at home and she filled in the gap for us.

The meal she brought was so delicious that we called her on the phone later in the day to request the meal's recipe long after she'd left. She not only gave us the recipe, she offered to take me to the store where she got the ingredients for the meal from and literally showed me all the aisles for each item. This has become a regular meal on my family menu list ever since.

Dawnetta's heart of gold manifested again when my mother-in-law visited us. We shared with Dawnetta how excited we were to host our expected guest. She asked to know her name and the date she was visiting. We shared the information with her, but we never knew she had a plan.

A day prior to my mother-in-law's visit, Dawnetta showed up at our door with her daughter Rachel and her grandson Jack with several decorating items. They decorated the house, the driveway and the lawn with several colorful ribbons and artworks as well as decorative cardboards on which my mother-in-law's name was designed with different welcome messages. We were all thrilled and surprised by Dawnetta's display of kindness and selflessness.

Some time ago, at a fund-raising event, I saw a fun-looking workshop stand kind of product for kids. The product caught my interest and I planned on bidding for it. Dave and Dawnetta were also at the event. They beat me to my plan, won the bid, got the item, paid for it and left.

My conclusion was that they wanted it for one of their grandkids as much as I wanted it for my son. I really didn't realize they already noticed my interest in getting the product. It touched my heart when they showed up at our door in their truck to deliver the same product to us.

How more kind can people possibly be? Yet, we are not of the same race. If everyone we see everywhere we all go were exactly like Dave and Dawnetta, a world devoid of racism and tribalism would be guaranteed and peace would reign throughout the nooks and crannies of our world.

CHAPTER 23:
THE POWER OF KINDNESS

Be kind to one another.

–Ellen DeGeneres

Ellen DeGeneres is one selfless lady with a heart of gold. At different times, she has touched numerous people across all races in the most positive manner. She has not only touched people with her hands, she has, indeed, touched the human race with her heart. By now, she should have won a Nobel Price for Kindness if such a category exists. However, it's really obvious that she does not do all that she does in expectation of some kind of gratification. She is, by all standards, a successful celebrity and a talk show host who has perfectly utilized a talk show tool on national television to put smiles on the faces of people across all races.

Ellen's crusade of kindness always resonates well with me, as I believe it does with millions of people. Over the years, she has skillfully combined the art of comedy with pleasant surprises and an unbelievable heart of kindness to lift several people above the troubled sea of life. She achieves this by helping to make people's dreams come true, raising people's hopes with broad smiles through life-changing gifts and donations. In line with her daily message of kindness, the beneficiaries of her largesse are not limited to a specific race, they are everyday people across the board—an act that complies with her "be kind to one another" statement. That statement has, over the years, become a crusade and a movement of a sort. Personally, I call her Ellen the Generous and I often wish there were more people like her who are driven by genuine desire to douse the tension of racism and erase the scourge of tribalism.

Like Ellen, some of the celebrities who are huge on give-back and whose give-back initiatives and individual social responsibility cut across all races include Tyler Perry, Akon, Steve Harvey, Lady Gaga, Jamie Foxx, Leonardo DiCaprio, Bill and Melinda Gates, Mel Gibson, Will and Jada Smith, Taylor Swift, Sandra Bullock, Morgan Freeman, George Clooney, Jay-Z and Beyoncé, Oprah Winfrey and others.

Ellen seems to be in a world of her own. She's just a kind-hearted human who uses every opportunity to preach kindness. Her daily crusade of kindness to one another may have yielded a lot of positive results that haven't been documented yet.

It is only that kind of crusade, and a similar belief in the ability of kindness and love to heal our world, that could produce the story of Dr. Sarah Schecter of the Oakridge School in Texas. While Ellen uses the tool of a talk show on national television as a platform to propagate her crusade of kindness, Sarah decides to utilize the platform available to her—the classroom.

Amazingly, the Oakridge School believes in the concepts of giving, love and kindness, which represent some of the core values that every student takes away from their regular academic classes and student-leadership training. These are specifically designed just so the students, having learned these concepts, become good ambassadors for their families, the school and themselves in the real world after their high-school education.

Dr. Sarah Schecter, as one of the facilitators of these concepts in the classrooms, happens to personally believe in these concepts herself. So Oakridge School and her are more like two of a kind with one common goal that forms the pivot upon which their strong bond swings.

Sarah works with the school kids on a daily basis and never minces words telling them the importance of love and kindness. She also teaches them how to love and show kindness as well. Since Oakridge School already presents the right atmosphere to introduce the most effective tool needed to ensure global peace to the kids, Sarah, in turn, makes herself available to help navigate the kids' ship in the right direction.

All of a sudden, there was a storm right in the middle of Sarah's navigation. It was an unexpected turbulence that threatened to rip the ship apart. As a matter of fact, it was a terrible situation that could potentially wreck the ship and permanently rest its main components at the bottom of the ocean. At this point, the survival of the ship along with the kids aboard depended solely on Sarah's navigation ability—a test of her expertise.

In the real world, it was actually a test of Sarah's crusade and teachings of love and kindness. It all started with a simple conversation with a lady named Amenze, mother of three of the kids at Oakridge School. One or two of her kids may have passed through the lower school where Sarah is a principal. Sarah knows her students very well, but she obviously doesn't know their parents as well as she does her students. So that fateful day when she saw Amenze on the school premises, her instincts told her all was not well with her. Out of care, and in the spirit of kindness, Sarah asked if everything was OK with her. Amenze nodded in the affirmative in a way that suggested all was well, but not too well after all.

In the course of discussion, Amenze opened up to Sarah. She'd been going through a lot on the home front. Nathaniel, her husband, was right on the verge of losing his life. He had a health condition and hope of survival diminished as each day rolled by. It was renal failure, and his kidney was failing fast. If there was a tiny hope for Nathaniel to live, that tiny hope became tinier with no assurance of remedy from the medical team unless a donor showed up.

For Amenze and Nathaniel, with the incessant dialysis appointments and the endless wait on the list of victims at the mercy of donors, it was a race of hope versus hopelessness. But unfortunately, hopelessness seemed to be winning the race and that meant one thing for Nathaniel: death. He may have fought several battles associated with living life before now, but none was as fierce as when death stared at him and looked straight into his eyes waiting to strike—possibly at the next blink.

Sarah showed a great deal of sympathy for what Amenze and Nathaniel were going through as a family. She gave Amenze some words of encouragement—which was the nicest and the kindest thing a nice and a kind person could do. They both went their different ways afterwards.

Incredibly, out of sight is never out of mind for Sarah. She couldn't stop thinking about Nathaniel. Despite the fact that she really didn't know them that much, she just couldn't stop wishing them well in her mind. As she wished them well in her mind, she felt very strongly that the family needed more than a mere wish—a timely action was needed to complement the good wishes as a matter of urgency.

Nathaniel's situation didn't get any better. His dying life would flash before his eyes every now and then. He would think about his wife having to deal with raising the kids all by herself and the kids growing up without their dear father. He thought very deeply and was disturbed about the fact that the kids were right on the verge of experiencing what it is like to grow up without a father.

Just as he was about to accept his fate, something happened on the other side of the city that was unexpected good news for the family. Someone volunteered and offered to donate a kidney to revive Nathaniel. It was the same Dr. Sarah Schecter, the principal of the school Nathaniel's kids attended.

Nathaniel's situation was a true "practice what you preach" test for Sarah. Amazingly, Sarah passed the test. She proved to the students and the entire world that she's not just paying lip service to the concept of kindness each time she teaches the kids about it. She sprang into action by indicating her willingness to redeem Nathaniel from an untimely death that was imminent. When her kidney was confirmed to be a perfect match, Sarah didn't change her mind. There was no looking back. She was all in and followed through the stages of the medical process to the last stage of surgery.

Sarah went above and beyond everyday kindness—she donated her kidney to Nathaniel, a total stranger. That kind gesture saved Nathaniel's life. Yet, Sarah and Nathaniel are not of the same race. What an incredible display of kindness. What an amazing display of selflessness. Imagine a world filled with schools like Oakridge. Imagine a world filled with the likes of Sarah. Imagine the depth of peace there would be.

Sarah has not only become a formidable force in the history of kindness, she has also engraved her footprint on the map of kindness as she adds her voice to the voices of great peace-loving individuals who have made history by advocating for service to humanity, self-lessness, love, unity among humans and kindness as the right paths to global peace.

One of such leading voices was that of Charles Chaplin. Sir Charles Spencer Chaplin, popularly known as Charlie Chaplin, was a comic actor and filmmaker who became a global icon in the silent film era. In his first dialogue film, a satire titled *The Great Dictator*, Chaplin played a dual role of a young Jewish barber as well as Hynkel, a dictator who was the ruler of Tomainia. After being mistaken for Hynkel, the dictator, the young Jewish barber, at the end of the film, called for a sustainable truce and global peace in this speech:

I'm sorry, but I don't want to be an emperor. That's not my business. I don't want to rule or conquer anyone. I should like to help everyone—if possible—Jew, Gentile, black man, white. We all want to help one another. Human beings are like that. We want to live by each other's happiness—not by each other's misery. We don't want to hate and despise one another. In this world there is room for everyone. And the good earth is rich and can provide for everyone. The way of life can be free and beautiful, but we have lost the way.

Greed has poisoned men's souls, has barricaded the world with hate, has goose-stepped us into misery and bloodshed. We have developed speed, but we have shut ourselves in. Machinery that gives abundance has left us in want. Our knowledge has made us cynical. Our cleverness, hard and unkind. We think too much and feel too little. More than machinery, we need humanity. More than cleverness, we need kindness and gentleness. Without these qualities, life will be violent and all will be lost....

The aeroplane and the radio have brought us closer together. The very nature of these inventions cries out for the goodness in men—cries out for universal brotherhood—for the unity of us all. Even now my voice is reaching millions throughout the world—millions of despairing men, women, and little children—victims of a system that makes men torture and imprison innocent people.

To those who can hear me, I say—do not despair. The misery that is now upon us is but the passing of greed—the bitterness of men who fear the way of human progress. The hate of men will pass, and dictators die, and the power they took from the people will return to the people. And so long as men die, liberty will never perish....

Soldiers! Don't give yourselves to brutes—men who despise you—enslave you—who regiment your lives—tell you what to do—what to think and what to feel! Who drill you— diet you—treat you like cattle, use you as cannon fodder. Don't give yourselves to these unnatural men—machine men with machine minds and machine hearts! You are not machines! You are not cattle! You are men! You have the love of humanity in your hearts! You don't hate! Only the unloved hate—the unloved and the unnatural! Soldiers! Don't fight for slavery! Fight for liberty!

In the 17th Chapter of St Luke it is written: "The Kingdom of God is within man" —not one man nor a group of men, but in all men! In you! You, the people have the power— the power to create machines. The power to create happiness!

You, the people, have the power to make this life free and beautiful, to make this life a wonderful adventure.

Then—in the name of democracy—let us use that power— let us all unite. Let us fight for a new world—a decent world that will give men a chance to work—that will give youth a future and old age a security. By the promise of these things, brutes have risen to power. But they lie! They do not fulfil that promise. They never will!

Dictators free themselves but they enslave the people! Now let us fight to fulfil that promise! Let us fight to free the world—to do away with national barriers—to do away with greed, with hate and intolerance. Let us fight for a world of reason, a world where science and progress will lead to all men's happiness. Soldiers! In the name of democracy, let us all unite!

Ironically, this 1940 speech is no doubt even more relevant in today's world. One can only imagine the tremendous tranquility, the level of harmony, and the depth of peace the entire world would experience if world leaders swallowed their pride, paid less attention to the power tussle for superlative military ranking and embraced all the peace-inclined suggestions, as well as the clarion calls for global unity in this speech.

For once, let's all take a break from wars, racism, tribalism, ethnicity, selfishness, hate, animosity, vindictiveness, anger, bitterness and prejudice and try love in a bid to experiencing how sweet peace is. Ellen DeGeneres may have envisioned what global peace would be like if we all inculcate a habit of kindness. As she always says at the end of her shows, "Be kind to one another."

REFERENCES

U.S. Office of Personnel Management. https://www.opm.gov/forms/ pdf_fill/sf181.pdf. Guide to Personnel Data Standards. Accessed 10 January 2020.

Live Science. https://www.livescience.com/worst-epidemics-and-pan-demics-in-history.html. Accessed 16 January 2020.

City of St. Louis. https://www.stlouis-mo.gov/government/depart-ments/planning/cultural-resources/preservation-plan/Part-I-African-American-Experience.cfm. Accessed 16 January, 2020.

American Association for the Advancement of Science/Science Mag. https://www.sciencemag.org/news/2020/04/how-does-corona-virus-kill-clinicians-trace- ferocious-rampage-through-body-brain-toes. Accessed 26 June 2020.

The Planetary Society. http://www.planetary.org/explore/space-top-ics/earth/pale-blue-dot.html. Accessed 10 March 2019.

Federal Character Commission. https://federalcharacter.gov.ng/. Accessed 18 June 2019.

ABOUT THE AUTHOR

Humanitarian, creative writer and data integration specialist, Adeleke Adefioye has always shown a genuine interest in human welfare. He is passionate about humanity, justice, equity and fairness. As a fresh college graduate serving his home country Nigeria, he won a Commendation Award as the most responsible and the most constructive corps member as well as a Merit Award as the most outstanding corps member.

Shortly after college, he started his first career as a broadcaster with a state-owned television station where he worked as a talk show host, studio continuity announcer and newscaster. He later moved to the print media having discovered that he couldn't suppress his instinctive aptitude for writing. As a journalist, he wrote extensively on politics, information technology, business and energy (power/oil and gas).

However, he changed career having successfully completed an MBA degree upon relocation to the United States of America. As an astute team player, he won the maiden edition of a firm-wide Slayer Award at the financial firm he currently works for.

In 2020, Ade, as he is fondly called by friends and colleagues, was nominated to The National Society of Leadership and Success by the University of Phoenix. His inordinate desire is to see a world with improved standard of living for all humans and a world where all races and nationalities coexist peacefully.